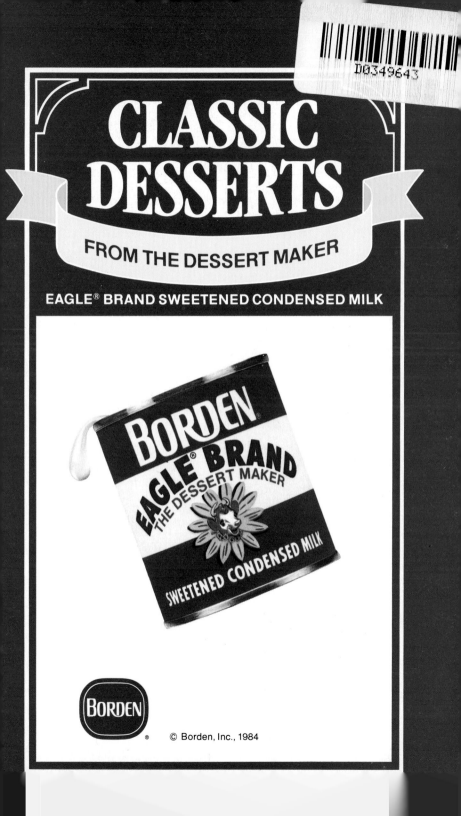

CLASSIC DESSERTS

FROM THE DESSERT MAKER

EAGLE® BRAND SWEETENED CONDENSED MILK

Dessert—that something special to deliciously complete the meal, satisfy a sweet tooth, savor with a cold glass of milk, a cup of steaming coffee or a sparkling glass of champagne.

For more than 125 years, Eagle® Brand Sweetened Condensed Milk has been the classic dessert maker for American consumers. Its creamy rich goodness has enhanced traditional desserts from candies, custards and cookies to ice creams, cheesecakes and pies. From the earliest Borden recipe books and ads, we know that the cooks of 1918 were no different from us in the 1980's in our search for convenience and high quality.

That's why, at Borden today, we can say with pride that Eagle Brand is our oldest—and most contemporary—product.

And with the same pride and commitment to quality which Gail Borden demonstrated in developing sweetened condensed milk in 1856, we present this collection of *Classic Desserts* from The Dessert Maker, Eagle® Brand Sweetened Condensed Milk. Enjoy!

Annie Watts
Annie Watts
Director, Borden Kitchens

Pictured on the cover: New York Style Cheesecake, Lemon Meringue Pie, Layered Mint Chocolate Candy, Fruit Bon Bons, Scotchy Turtles, Triple Layer Cookie Bars, Peanut Blossoms, Mini Fruitcake Morsels

---

CREDITS:

Borden Kitchens:	Annie Watts Cloncs, Director
	Charlene Sneed, Senior Home Economist
Design and Production:	Mallard Marketing Associates, Inc.
	Betsy J. Nagle, Project Director
	Darcy W. Reber, Creative Coordinator
	Denny Knittig, Creative Director
	Donnie Flora, Food Stylist
	Glenn Peterson, Photographer
Color Separations:	Colorbrite, Inc.
Print Production:	The Lehigh Press, Inc.

CLASSIC DESSERTS

CONTENTS

THE DESSERT MAKER

I t's been called "magic" ... a can of Eagle® Brand Sweetened Condensed Milk plus a few select ingredients and the results are, well, like magic! Rich chocolate candies, moist cookie bars, picture-perfect lemon pies, light and luscious cheesecakes, fudgy frostings, caramel flans and creamy smooth ice cream ... just a few of the classic desserts made with Eagle Brand.

Try a Tasty Touch of Magic

10 Luscious Recipes Made Easy
With the Magic of Eagle® Brand
Sweetened Condensed Milk

BORDEN
EAGLE BRAND
SWEETENED CONDENSED MILK

MAGIC RECIPES

•

Quicker, easier surer to succeed

Did you ever hear of a lemon pie filling — creamy and lemon-y and smooth—that is made without cooking? See pages 28 to 31 for this and other truly amazing pie recipes.

A miracle here! Every lovely candy pictured at the right is made without going near a stove! See pages 32 to 34.

And who said ice cream making is lots of trouble? Expensive? Better see pages 15 to 17!

Around the turn of the century, good cooks everywhere began putting Eagle® Brand Sweetened Condensed Milk to work as a dessert maker. An all-natural pre-cooked blend of fresh whole milk and pure cane sugar, sweetened condensed milk blends almost magically with other ingredients. Because of this quality, preparation time is minimized. Most desserts made with sweetened condensed milk call for few ingredients, and many require little or no cooking.

The convenience and simplicity of cooking with sweetened condensed milk, as well as the delicious results, have confirmed Eagle Brand's place in history as a classic dessert maker. However, Gail Borden, who invented the product, had another idea in mind.

In the mid-1800's food poisoning and other illnesses related to lack of refrigeration and preservation techniques were common. Borden's concern with these problems led him to the development of sweetened condensed milk, a vacuum-cooked milk product that would not spoil when left unrefrigerated. He was granted a patent in 1856, and began selling his product from a push cart in New York. Later he called the product Eagle Brand after the American eagle, recognized as a symbol of pride and high quality.

The Civil War brought Eagle® Brand Sweetened Condensed Milk the recognition required to make it a household item. The military needed milk that would keep well, and Borden's product filled that need. It was publicly praised for saving many lives during that conflict.

Eagle Brand was also credited with significantly lowering the infant mortality rate throughout North America. Gail Borden's discovery provided a milk that would remain safe and wholesome —at that time, an important contribution to the nourishment of infants and children. Since then, other products have been developed which better meet the need for a healthful and nutritious baby formula.

In 1911 The Borden Company established its own "Welfare Department," the forerunner of today's Borden Kitchens. Then, as now, the department's efforts were focused on providing consumers with new ways to use sweetened condensed milk in preparing foods for their families. The cookbooks and magazine ads produced by the Borden Kitchens continue to provide contemporary Eagle Brand recipes and serving ideas for American consumers.

In the early 1900's sweetened condensed milk was used extensively as a creamer and sweetener for coffee, tea and cocoa. Ads of 1918 promised a flavor that makes "an early morning frown give way to an all-day smile of satisfaction."

The creamer-sweetener role has endured over the years, and in some parts of the country today, Eagle Brand always accompanies coffee for special guests in the home. In the Beverage section of this book, look for the delicious punches, shakes and drinks made with the rich creamy goodness of Eagle Brand.

The post World War I era brought prosperity to the country—and refrigeration to most kitchens. Eagle® Brand Sweetened Condensed Milk became increasingly popular as a recipe ingredient, especially for desserts.

Among the company's earliest recipe campaigns was one for

homemade ice cream made in the new "automatic" refrigerator. Vanilla, chocolate and strawberry were the favorite flavors then, as they are today.

The popularity and convenience of Eagle Brand as an ice cream ingredient has not changed. Many delicious recipes for creamy smooth ice creams and frozen desserts are featured in this book.

A 1927 Eagle Brand advertisement promised "glorious" pumpkin pie... "the kind about which poets have sung... the kind of pumpkin pie that cheats the divorce courts... pumpkin pie that has made America great!" Whether in pumpkin, chocolate or Cherry Cheese, Eagle Brand remains a key ingredient in "glorious" pies.

The same is true for all kinds of candies and confections where sweetened condensed milk is the rich creamy base for always-smooth foolproof fudge and chewy macaroons. Coconut Macaroons (spelled "cocoanut" in those days), when made with Eagle Brand, were described as "dainty bits of confection that a French pastry chef might well be proud of."

Recipes made with sweetened condensed milk were as easy to prepare then as they are today. Coconut Macaroons, for example, requires only four ingredients. Early Eagle Brand ice cream recipes called for four or five ingredients— the same as today's ice cream recipes. Magic Lemon Meringue Pie, called Lemon Icebox Pie by homemakers of the 1940's, is made with six ingredients, and cooking is required only to brown the meringue. This recipe favorite is presented here as Creamy Lemon Meringue Pie.

Another quick and easy all-time favorite is our Magic Cookie Bars. You may call these luscious chocolate-y cookies "Hello Dolly Bars" or "7-Layer Bars."

The search for cooking convenience was as strong in the mid-1900's as it is today. Borden cookbooks for Eagle® Brand Sweetened Condensed Milk promised convenience with names such as New Magic in the Kitchen, Magic! Amazing Shortcuts in Cooking and Borden's Eagle Brand Magic Recipes. Eagle Brand ads, as well as the cookbooks, offered convenient, easy recipes that could be "mixed up even by little girls playing with toy kitchens ... prepared by homemakers 20 minutes before guests arrived for tea ... appreciated by efficient women."

In 1931 a Borden Kitchens' promotion offered homemakers $25 for their original recipes. The rules called for "recipes in which Eagle Brand makes cooking quicker, easier, surer."

The response was tremendous! Consumers submitted over 80,000 recipes. Among those accepted as award winners were some whose unusual names evoke great curiosity as to their probable nature ... "Applelicious," "Caramel Lunchettes," "Magic Surprise," "Cellophane Loaf," "Enoch Sundae" and "Maple Cream Foundation."

Eagle® Brand Sweetened Condensed Milk continued to grow in popularity, gaining promotional assistance from Elsie the Borden Cow. Elsie made her debut in national consumer magazines in 1938 and starred in Borden's exhibit at the New York World's Fair the following year. She attended press parties, charity events and even a debutante ball.

Eventually Elsie replaced the American eagle as the featured logo on the sweetened condensed milk label. By the 1960's Elsie had become America's best known spokes-cow—a recognized symbol of wholesomeness and quality.

Elsie remains a familiar sight in kitchens today. Good cooks throughout the country continue to create desserts with sweetened condensed milk from the can bearing Elsie's image.

Classic Desserts

Over the years, many recipes using Eagle® Brand Sweetened Condensed Milk have become classics. Some were advertising features. Others were created by consumers. Still others were published in Borden cookbooks, dating back to the early 1900's.

The Borden Kitchens has selected the best of these favorites and developed exciting new recipes to create this cookbook. All the recipes were carefully tested in the Borden Kitchens to assure the consistent quality and good taste you've come to expect from Eagle Brand.

This cookbook salutes Eagle® Brand Sweetened Condensed Milk as the dessert maker... a product that has always provided consumers a convenient, easy way to create a wide variety of delicious Classic Desserts.

Pictured: Cherry Cheese Pie,
Fresh Fruit Cheese Pie,
Ambrosia Cheese Pie
(recipes page 14).

PIES

FROM THE DESSERT MAKER

CHERRY CHEESE PIE

Makes one 9-inch pie

1 (9-inch) baked pastry shell *or*
graham cracker crumb crust
1 (8-ounce) package cream
cheese, softened
1 (14-ounce) can Eagle® Brand
Sweetened Condensed Milk
(NOT evaporated milk)
⅓ cup ReaLemon® Lemon Juice
from Concentrate
1 teaspoon vanilla extract
1 (21-ounce) can cherry pie
filling, chilled

In large mixer bowl, beat cheese until
fluffy. Gradually beat in sweetened
condensed milk until smooth. Stir in
ReaLemon and vanilla. Pour into
prepared pastry shell. Chill 3 hours or
until set. Top with desired amount of
pie filling before serving. Refrigerate
leftovers.

Topping Variations:

Fresh Fruit: Omit cherry pie filling. Just
before serving, arrange well drained
fresh strawberries, banana slices
(dipped in ReaLemon and well drained)
and blueberries on top of chilled pie.
Just before serving, brush fruit with
light corn syrup if desired.

Ambrosia: Omit cherry pie filling. In
small saucepan, combine ½ cup peach
or apricot preserves, ¼ cup flaked
coconut, 2 tablespoons orange juice *or*
orange-flavored liqueur and 2 teaspoons cornstarch; cook and stir until
thickened. Remove from heat. Arrange
fresh orange sections over top of pie;
top with coconut mixture. Chill
thoroughly.

Blueberry: Omit cherry pie filling. In
medium saucepan, combine ¼ cup
sugar and 1 tablespoon cornstarch; mix
well. Add ½ cup water, 2 tablespoons
ReaLemon then 2 cups fresh or dry-
pack frozen blueberries, thawed; mix
well. Bring to a boil; reduce heat and
simmer 3 minutes or until thick and
clear. Cool 10 minutes. Spread over
pie. Chill thoroughly.

Continued next column

Cherry Cheese Pie Topping Variations:

Cranberry: Omit cherry pie filling. In
medium saucepan, combine ⅓ cup
sugar and 1 tablespoon cornstarch.
Add ½ cup plus 2 tablespoons cold
water and 2 cups fresh or dry-pack
frozen cranberries; mix well. Bring to a
boil; reduce heat and simmer 10 minutes,
stirring constantly. Cool 15 minutes.
Spread over pie. Chill thoroughly.

IMPOSSIBLE PIE

Makes one 10-inch pie

1 (14-ounce) can Eagle® Brand
Sweetened Condensed Milk
(NOT evaporated milk)
1½ cups water
½ cup biscuit baking mix
3 eggs
¼ cup margarine or butter,
softened
1½ teaspoons vanilla extract
1 cup flaked coconut

Preheat oven to 350° In blender
container, combine all ingredients
except coconut. Blend on low speed
3 minutes. Pour mixture into buttered
10-inch pie plate; let stand 5 minutes.
Sprinkle coconut over top. Carefully
place in oven; bake 35 to 40 minutes or
until knife inserted near edge comes
out clean. Cool slightly; serve warm or
cool. Refrigerate leftovers.

Tip: Pie can be baked in buttered 9-inch
pie plate but it will be extremely full.

FUDGY PECAN PIE ▲

Makes one 9-inch pie

1 (9-inch) unbaked pastry shell
1 (4-ounce) package sweet
    cooking chocolate *or* 2
    (1-ounce) squares un-
    sweetened chocolate
¼ cup margarine or butter
1 (14-ounce) can Eagle® Brand
    Sweetened Condensed Milk
    (NOT evaporated milk)
½ cup hot water
2 eggs, well beaten
1 teaspoon vanilla extract
⅛ teaspoon salt
1¼ cups pecan halves or pieces

Preheat oven to 350°. In medium
saucepan, over low heat, melt chocolate
with margarine. Stir in sweetened
condensed milk, hot water and eggs;
mix well. Remove from heat; stir in
remaining ingredients. Pour into
prepared pastry shell. Bake 40 to 45
minutes or until center is set. Cool
slightly. Serve warm or chilled. Garnish
as desired. Refrigerate leftovers.

FUDGE DELUXE PIE

Makes one 9-inch pie

1 (9-inch) baked pastry shell
3 (1-ounce) squares semi-sweet
    or unsweetened chocolate
1 (14-ounce) can Eagle® Brand
    Sweetened Condensed Milk
    (NOT evaporated milk)
¼ teaspoon salt
¼ cup hot water
1 teaspoon vanilla extract
1 cup (½ pint) whipping cream

In heavy saucepan, over medium heat,
melt chocolate with sweetened condensed milk and salt. Cook and stir until
very thick and fudgy, 5 to 8 minutes.
Add water; cook and stir until mixture
thickens and boils. Remove from heat;
stir in vanilla. Cool 15 minutes. Chill
thoroughly, 20 to 30 minutes; stir. In
large mixer bowl, beat whipping cream
until stiff; fold in cooled chocolate
mixture. Pour into prepared pastry
shell. Chill 3 hours or until set. Garnish
as desired. Refrigerate leftovers.

◄ CREAMY LEMON MERINGUE PIE

Makes one 8- or 9-inch pie

1 (8- or 9-inch) baked pastry shell or graham cracker crumb crust
3 eggs*, separated
1 (14-ounce) can Eagle® Brand Sweetened Condensed Milk (NOT evaporated milk)
½ cup ReaLemon® Lemon Juice from Concentrate
Few drops yellow food coloring, optional
¼ teaspoon cream of tartar
⅓ cup sugar

Preheat oven to 350°. In medium mixing bowl, beat egg yolks; stir in sweetened condensed milk, ReaLemon and food coloring if desired. Pour into prepared pastry shell. In small mixer bowl, beat egg whites with cream of tartar until soft peaks form; gradually add sugar, beating until stiff but not dry. Spread meringue on top of pie, sealing carefully to edge of shell. Bake 12 to 15 minutes or until golden brown. Cool. Chill thoroughly. Refrigerate leftovers.

LEMON CHIFFON PIE

Makes one 8- or 9-inch pie

1 (8- or 9-inch) graham cracker crumb crust
1 (14-ounce) can Eagle® Brand Sweetened Condensed Milk (NOT evaporated milk)
⅓ cup ReaLemon® Lemon Juice from Concentrate
Few drops yellow food coloring, optional
3 egg whites*
¼ teaspoon cream of tartar

In medium mixing bowl, combine sweetened condensed milk, ReaLemon and food coloring if desired; mix well. In small mixer bowl, beat egg whites with cream of tartar until stiff but not dry; gently fold into sweetened condensed milk mixture. Pour into prepared crust. Chill 3 hours or until set. Refrigerate leftovers.

*Use only Grade A clean, uncracked eggs.

LEMON ICEBOX PIE

Makes one 9-inch pie

1½ cups vanilla wafer crumbs (about 40 wafers)
¼ cup margarine or butter, melted
1 envelope unflavored gelatine
1¾ cups water
1 (14-ounce) can Eagle® Brand Sweetened Condensed Milk (NOT evaporated milk)
1 (3-ounce) package or 6 tablespoons Wyler's® Presweetened Lemonade Flavor Drink Crystals

Combine crumbs and margarine; press firmly on bottom and up side of 9-inch pie plate. Chill. Meanwhile, in small saucepan, sprinkle gelatine over ¼ cup water; let stand 1 minute. Over low heat, stir until gelatine dissolves; set aside. In medium mixing bowl, combine sweetened condensed milk, remaining 1½ cups water and lemonade crystals; mix well. Stir in gelatine mixture. Pour into prepared crust. Chill at least 3 hours or until set. Garnish as desired. Refrigerate leftovers.

PINK LEMONADE PIE

Makes one 8- or 9-inch pie

1 (8- or 9-inch) baked pastry shell
1 (6-ounce) can frozen pink lemonade concentrate, thawed
1 (8-ounce) package cream cheese, softened
1 (14-ounce) can Eagle® Brand Sweetened Condensed Milk (NOT evaporated milk)
Few drops red food coloring, optional
1 (4-ounce) container frozen nondairy whipped topping, thawed
½ cup pink tinted coconut*

In large mixer bowl, beat cheese until fluffy; gradually beat in sweetened condensed milk then lemonade concentrate and food coloring if desired. Fold in whipped topping. Pour into prepared pastry shell. Chill 4 hours or until set. Garnish with coconut. Refrigerate leftovers.

*See page 122.

17

Traditional Pumpkin Pie · Sour Cream Topped Pumpkin Pie

TRADITIONAL PUMPKIN PIE

Makes one 9-inch pie

1 (9-inch) unbaked pastry shell
1 (16-ounce) can pumpkin (about 2 cups)
1 (14-ounce) can Eagle® Brand Sweetened Condensed Milk (NOT evaporated milk)
2 eggs
1 teaspoon ground cinnamon
½ teaspoon ground ginger
½ teaspoon ground nutmeg
½ teaspoon salt

Preheat oven to 425°. In large mixer bowl, combine all ingredients except pastry shell; mix well. Pour into prepared pastry shell. Bake 15 minutes. Reduce oven temperature to 350°; continue baking 35 to 40 minutes or until knife inserted 1 inch from edge comes out clean. Cool. Garnish as desired. Refrigerate leftovers.

Continued next column

Traditional Pumpkin Pie Topping Variations:

Sour Cream Topping: In medium mixing bowl, combine 1½ cups sour cream, 2 tablespoons sugar and 1 teaspoon vanilla extract. After 30 minutes of baking, spread evenly over top of pie; bake 10 minutes longer. Garnish as desired.

Streusel Topping: In medium mixing bowl, combine ½ cup firmly packed light brown sugar and ½ cup unsifted flour; cut in ¼ cup cold margarine or butter until crumbly. Stir in ¼ cup chopped nuts. After 30 minutes of baking, sprinkle on top of pie; bake 10 minutes longer.

Streusel Topped Pumpkin Pie

LUSCIOUS SWEET POTATO PIE

Makes one 9-inch pie

1 (9-inch) unbaked pastry shell
1 pound (2 medium) yams or
   sweet potatoes, cooked and
   peeled
½ cup margarine or butter,
   softened
1 (14-ounce) can Eagle® Brand
   Sweetened Condensed Milk
   (NOT evaporated milk)
¼ cup orange-flavored liqueur
   or 2 teaspoons grated
   orange rind
1 teaspoon ground cinnamon
½ teaspoon ground nutmeg
¼ teaspoon salt
2 eggs

Preheat oven to 350°. In large mixer
bowl, mash yams with margarine; add
remaining ingredients except pastry
shell and eggs. Beat until mixture is
smooth and well blended. Stir in eggs.
Pour into prepared pastry shell. Bake
50 to 55 minutes or until knife inserted
near center comes out clean. Cool.
Refrigerate leftovers.

Tip: 1 (16- or 17-ounce) can sweet
potatoes or yams can be substituted for
fresh. Melt margarine. Proceed as above.

SPIRITED ALOHA CREAM PIE

Makes one 9-inch pie

2½ cups flaked coconut, toasted
⅓ cup margarine or butter, melted
1 (8-ounce) package cream
   cheese, softened
1 (14-ounce) can Eagle® Brand
   Sweetened Condensed Milk
   (NOT evaporated milk)
1 (6-ounce) can frozen pineapple-
   orange juice concentrate,
   thawed
1 (8-ounce) can crushed
   pineapple, well drained
3 tablespoons light rum
1 tablespoon orange-flavored
   liqueur
1 cup (½ pint) whipping cream,
   whipped

Combine coconut and margarine; press
firmly on bottom and up side to rim of
9-inch pie plate. Chill. Meanwhile, in
large mixer bowl, beat cheese until
fluffy. Gradually beat in sweetened
condensed milk then juice concentrate
until smooth. Stir in pineapple, rum and
liqueur. Fold in whipped cream. Pour
into prepared crust. Chill 6 hours or
until set. Garnish as desired. Refrigerate
leftovers.

MILLION DOLLAR PIES

Makes two 8-inch pies

2 (8-inch) prepared graham
    cracker crumb crusts
1 (3½-ounce) can flaked coconut
    (1⅓ cups)
1 (14-ounce) can Eagle® Brand
    Sweetened Condensed Milk
    (NOT evaporated milk)
1 (20-ounce) can juice-pack
    crushed pineapple *or* 1 (29-
    ounce) can fruit cocktail, *well
    drained*
1 cup coarsely chopped pecans
¼ cup ReaLemon® Lemon Juice
    from Concentrate
1 (8-ounce) container frozen
    non-dairy whipped topping,
    thawed

Toast ⅓ *cup* coconut; set aside. In large
mixing bowl, combine sweetened
condensed milk, pineapple, remaining
1 cup coconut, pecans and ReaLemon;
mix well. Fold in whipped topping. Pour
into prepared crusts. Garnish with
toasted coconut. Chill 3 hours or until
set. Refrigerate leftovers.

Million Dollar Dessert Squares: In
medium mixing bowl, combine ½ cup
margarine or butter, melted, 1¼ cups
graham cracker crumbs and ¼ cup
sugar; mix well. Press firmly on bottom
of 13x9-inch baking pan. Chill. Prepare
filling as directed. Spread filling
mixture evenly over crust. Top with
toasted coconut. Chill as above.

FRESH FRUIT DESSERT PIZZA

Makes one 12-inch pie

1 (14-ounce) can Eagle® Brand
    Sweetened Condensed Milk
    (NOT evaporated milk)
½ cup sour cream
¼ cup ReaLemon® Lemon Juice
    from Concentrate
1 teaspoon vanilla extract
½ cup margarine or butter,
    softened
¼ cup firmly packed light brown
    sugar
1 cup unsifted flour
¼ cup quick-cooking oats
¼ cup finely chopped walnuts
    Assorted fresh or canned fruit
    (strawberries, grapes, kiwi-
    fruit, orange, pineapple,
    banana, etc.)

Preheat oven to 375°. In medium
mixing bowl, combine sweetened
condensed milk, sour cream, ReaLemon
and vanilla; mix well. Chill. In large
mixer bowl, beat margarine and sugar
until fluffy; add flour, oats and walnuts.
Mix well. On lightly greased pizza pan
or baking sheet, press dough into
12-inch circle forming rim around edge.
Prick with fork. Bake 10 to 12 minutes
or until golden brown. Cool. Spoon
filling evenly over crust. Arrange fruit
on top. Chill before serving. Refrigerate
leftovers.

BANANA SPLIT DESSERT PIZZA

Makes one 12-inch pie

- 1 (14-ounce) can Eagle® Brand Sweetened Condensed Milk (NOT evaporated milk)
- ½ cup sour cream
- 6 tablespoons ReaLemon® Lemon Juice from Concentrate
- 1 teaspoon vanilla extract
- ½ cup margarine or butter, softened
- ¼ cup firmly packed brown sugar
- 1 cup unsifted flour
- ¾ cup chopped nuts
- 3 medium bananas, sliced
- 1 (1-ounce) square semi-sweet chocolate
- 1 tablespoon margarine or butter
- 1 (8-ounce) can sliced pineapple, drained and cut in half
  Maraschino cherries and nuts

Continued next column

Banana Split Dessert Pizza

Preheat oven to 375°. In medium mixing bowl, combine sweetened condensed milk, sour cream, ¼ cup ReaLemon and vanilla; mix well. Chill. In large mixer bowl, beat margarine and sugar until fluffy; add flour and ¾ cup nuts. Mix well. On lightly greased pizza pan or baking sheet, press dough into 12-inch circle forming rim around edge. Prick with fork. Bake 10 to 12 minutes or until golden brown. Cool. Arrange 2 bananas on cooled crust. Spoon filling evenly over bananas. Dip remaining banana slices in remaining *2 tablespoons* ReaLemon; arrange on top along with pineapple, cherries and additional nuts. In small saucepan, over low heat, melt chocolate with margarine; drizzle over pie. Chill thoroughly. Refrigerate leftovers.

Tip: Crust and filling can be made in advance and held until ready to assemble. Cover crust and store at room temperature; store filling in refrigerator.

STREUSEL-TOPPED APPLE CUSTARD PIE

Makes one 9-inch pie

1 (9-inch) unbaked pastry shell
4 large all-purpose apples, pared
  and sliced (about 4 cups)
2 eggs
1 (14-ounce) can Eagle® Brand
  Sweetened Condensed Milk
  (NOT evaporated milk)
¼ cup margarine or butter, melted
½ teaspoon ground cinnamon
  Dash ground nutmeg
½ cup firmly packed light brown
  sugar
½ cup unsifted flour
¼ cup cold margarine or butter
¼ cup chopped nuts

Preheat oven to 425°. Arrange apples in prepared pastry shell. In medium mixing bowl, beat eggs. Add sweetened condensed milk, margarine, cinnamon and nutmeg; mix well. Pour over apples. In medium mixing bowl, combine sugar and flour; cut in margarine until crumbly. Stir in nuts. Sprinkle over pie. Place in bottom third of oven; bake 10 minutes. Reduce oven temperature to 375°; continue baking 35 to 40 minutes or until golden brown. Cool. Refrigerate leftovers.

Peach Variation: Omit apples. Substitute 1 (29-ounce) can sliced peaches, well drained, for apples. Proceed as above.

CANDY APPLE CHEESE PIE

Makes one 9-inch pie

1 (9-inch) baked pastry shell
1 (8-ounce) package cream
  cheese, softened
1 (14-ounce) can Eagle® Brand
  Sweetened Condensed Milk
  (NOT evaporated milk)
⅓ cup ReaLemon® Lemon Juice
  from Concentrate
1 teaspoon vanilla extract
1 (20-ounce) can pie sliced
  apples, *well drained* on
  paper towels
¼ cup red cinnamon candies
6 tablespoons water
2 teaspoons cornstarch

In large mixer bowl, beat cheese until fluffy. Gradually beat in sweetened condensed milk until smooth. Stir in ReaLemon and vanilla. Pour into prepared pastry shell. Arrange apple slices on top; set aside. In small saucepan, over *low* heat, dissolve cinnamon candies in ¼ *cup* water. Stir together remaining *2 tablespoons* water and cornstarch; add to cinnamon mixture. Cook and stir until mixture thickens and boils. Remove from heat; cool slightly. Drizzle over apples. Chill 3 hours or until set. Refrigerate leftovers.

Pictured: Streusel-Topped Apple Custard Pie, Candy Apple Cheese Pie.

TROPICAL LIME PIE ▲

Makes one 9-inch pie

2½ cups flaked coconut, toasted
⅓ cup margarine or butter, melted
1 (8-ounce) package cream cheese, softened
1 (14-ounce) can Eagle® Brand Sweetened Condensed Milk (NOT evaporated milk)
⅓ cup ReaLime® Lime Juice from Concentrate
Few drops green food coloring, optional
1 (4-ounce) container frozen non-dairy whipped topping, thawed

Combine coconut and margarine; press firmly on bottom and up side to rim of 9-inch pie plate. Chill. Meanwhile, in large mixer bowl, beat cheese until fluffy. Gradually beat in sweetened condensed milk then ReaLime and food coloring if desired until smooth. Fold in whipped topping. Pour into prepared crust. Chill 3 hours or until set. Garnish as desired. Refrigerate leftovers.

KEY LIME PIE

Makes one 8- or 9-inch pie

1 (8- or 9-inch) baked pastry shell
3 eggs*, separated
1 (14-ounce) can Eagle® Brand Sweetened Condensed Milk (NOT evaporated milk)
½ cup ReaLime® Lime Juice from Concentrate
Few drops green food coloring, optional
½ teaspoon cream of tartar
⅓ cup sugar

Preheat oven to 350°. In medium mixing bowl, beat egg yolks; stir in sweetened condensed milk, ReaLime and food coloring if desired. Pour into prepared pastry shell. In small mixer bowl, beat egg whites with cream of tartar until soft peaks form; gradually add sugar, beating until stiff but not dry. Spread on top of pie, sealing carefully to edge of shell. Bake 12 to 15 minutes or until golden brown. Cool. Chill thoroughly. Refrigerate leftovers.

Tip: For a lighter filling, fold 1 stiffly beaten egg white into filling mixture; proceed as above.

*Use only Grade A clean, uncracked eggs.

FLUFFY ORANGE PIE

Makes one 9-inch pie

**2 cups vanilla wafer crumbs
  (about 50 wafers)**
⅓ cup margarine or butter, melted
**1 (8-ounce) package cream
  cheese, softened**
**1 (14-ounce) can Eagle® Brand
  Sweetened Condensed Milk
  (NOT evaporated milk)**
**1 (6-ounce) can frozen orange
  juice concentrate, thawed**
**1 cup (½ pint) whipping cream,
  whipped**

Combine crumbs and margarine; press firmly on bottom and up side of 9-inch pie plate. Chill. Meanwhile, in large mixer bowl, beat cheese until fluffy; gradually beat in sweetened condensed milk then juice concentrate until smooth. Fold in whipped cream. Pile into crust. Chill 2 hours or until set. Garnish as desired. Refrigerate leftovers.

AVOCADO CHEESE PIE

Makes one 9-inch pie

**1 (9-inch) graham cracker crumb
  crust**
**1 (8-ounce) package cream
  cheese, softened**
**1 (14-ounce) can Eagle® Brand
  Sweetened Condensed Milk
  (NOT evaporated milk)**
**1 ripe medium avocado, mashed
  or pureed (about ½ cup)**
**½ cup ReaLime® Lime Juice from
  Concentrate**
¼ teaspoon salt
**Few drops green food coloring,
  optional**
Whipped cream, optional

In large mixer bowl, beat cheese until fluffy. Gradually beat in sweetened condensed milk then avocado, ReaLime, salt and food coloring if desired until smooth. Pour into prepared crust. Chill 4 hours or until set. Garnish with whipped cream if desired. Refrigerate leftovers.

Fluffy Orange Pie

◄ MINI FRUIT CHEESE TARTS

Makes 24 tarts

24 (2- or 3-inch) prepared tart-size
    crusts
1 (8-ounce) package cream
    cheese, softened
1 (14-ounce) can Eagle® Brand
    Sweetened Condensed Milk
    (NOT evaporated milk)
⅓ cup ReaLemon® Lemon Juice
    from Concentrate
1 teaspoon vanilla extract
    Assorted fruit (strawberries,
    blueberries, bananas, rasp-
    berries, orange segments,
    cherries, kiwifruit, grapes,
    pineapple, etc.)
¼ cup apple jelly, melted

In large mixer bowl, beat cheese until
fluffy. Gradually beat in sweetened
condensed milk until smooth. Stir in
ReaLemon and vanilla. Spoon equal
portions into crusts. Top with fruit;
brush with jelly. Chill thoroughly.
Refrigerate leftovers.

CREAMY MOCK CHEESE PIE

Makes one 8- or 9-inch pie

1 (8- or 9-inch) graham cracker
    crumb crust
1 (16-ounce) container sour
    cream
1 (14-ounce) can Eagle® Brand
    Sweetened Condensed Milk
    (NOT evaporated milk)
3 tablespoons (1 scoop) Wyler's®
    Presweetened Lemonade
    Flavor Drink Crystals
    Peach preserves, optional

Preheat oven to 350°. In medium
mixing bowl, combine sour cream,
sweetened condensed milk and
lemonade crystals; mix well. Pour into
prepared crust. Bake 25 to 30 minutes.
Cool thoroughly. Chill at least 2 hours.
Garnish with preserves if desired.
Refrigerate leftovers.

Tip: Other fruit preserves can be
substituted for peach preserves.

COCONUT CUSTARD PIE

Makes one 9-inch pie

- 1 (9-inch) unbaked pastry shell
- 1 cup flaked coconut
- 3 eggs
- 1 (14-ounce) can Eagle® Brand Sweetened Condensed Milk (NOT evaporated milk)
- 1¼ cups hot water
- 1 teaspoon vanilla extract
- ¼ teaspoon salt
- ⅛ teaspoon ground nutmeg

Preheat oven to 425°. Toast ½ cup coconut; set aside. Bake pastry shell 8 minutes; cool slightly. Meanwhile, in medium mixing bowl, beat eggs. Add sweetened condensed milk, water, vanilla, salt and nutmeg; mix well. Stir in remaining ½ cup coconut. Pour into prepared pastry shell. Sprinkle with toasted coconut. Bake 10 minutes. Reduce oven temperature to 350°; continue baking 25 to 30 minutes or until knife inserted near center comes out clean. Cool. Chill if desired. Refrigerate leftovers.

Custard Pie: Omit coconut. Proceed as above.

Coconut Custard Pie

CHOCOLATE CUSTARD PIE

Makes one 9-inch pie

- 1 (9-inch) unbaked pastry shell
- 2 (1-ounce) squares semi-sweet chocolate
- 1 (14-ounce) can Eagle® Brand Sweetened Condensed Milk (NOT evaporated milk)
- 3 eggs, well beaten
- 1½ cups *hot* water
- 2 teaspoons vanilla extract
- 1 (4-ounce) container frozen non-dairy whipped topping, thawed

Preheat oven to 425°. In heavy saucepan, over low heat, melt chocolate with sweetened condensed milk. Stir in eggs; mix well. Add hot water and vanilla; mix well. Pour into prepared pastry shell. Bake 10 minutes. Reduce oven temperature to 300°; continue baking 25 to 30 minutes or until knife inserted near center comes out clean. Cool. Chill thoroughly. Spread top with whipped topping. Refrigerate leftovers.

CRANBERRY CRUMB PIE ▲

Makes one 9-inch pie

1 (9-inch) unbaked pastry shell
1 (8-ounce) package cream
   cheese, softened
1 (14-ounce) can Eagle® Brand
   Sweetened Condensed Milk
   (NOT evaporated milk)
¼ cup ReaLemon® Lemon Juice
   from Concentrate
3 tablespoons light brown sugar
2 tablespoons cornstarch
1 (16-ounce) can whole berry
   cranberry sauce
¼ cup cold margarine or butter
⅓ cup unsifted flour
¾ cup chopped walnuts

Continued next column

Cranberry Crumb Pie

Preheat oven to 425°. Bake pastry shell 8 minutes; remove from oven. Reduce oven temperature to 375°. In large mixer bowl, beat cheese until fluffy. Gradually beat in sweetened condensed milk until smooth. Stir in ReaLemon. Pour into prepared pastry shell. In small bowl, combine *1 tablespoon* sugar and cornstarch; mix well. Stir in cranberry sauce. Spoon evenly over cheese mixture. In medium mixing bowl, cut margarine into flour and remaining *2 tablespoons* sugar until crumbly. Stir in nuts. Sprinkle evenly over cranberry mixture. Bake 45 to 50 minutes or until bubbly and golden. Cool. Serve at room temperature or chill thoroughly. Refrigerate leftovers.

SPIRITED EGG NOG CUSTARD PIE

Makes one 9-inch pie

- **1 (9-inch) unbaked pastry shell**
- **1 (14-ounce) can Eagle® Brand Sweetened Condensed Milk (NOT evaporated milk)**
- **1⅓ cups warm water**
- **2 tablespoons light rum**
- **1 tablespoon brandy**
- **1 teaspoon vanilla extract**
- **½ teaspoon ground nutmeg**
- **3 eggs, well beaten**

Continued next column

Spirited Egg Nog Custard Pie

Preheat oven to 425°. Bake pastry shell 8 minutes; remove from oven. In large mixing bowl, combine all ingredients except eggs; mix well. Stir in eggs. Pour into prepared pastry shell. Bake 10 minutes. Reduce oven temperature to 325°; continue baking 25 to 30 minutes or until knife inserted near center comes out clean. Cool. Chill if desired. Refrigerate leftovers.

GLAZED APPLE CREAM TART

Makes one 9-inch tart

½ cup plus 2 tablespoons
   margarine or butter, softened
¼ cup firmly packed light brown
   sugar
1 cup unsifted flour
¼ cup quick-cooking oats
¼ cup finely chopped walnuts
1 (14-ounce) can Eagle® Brand
   Sweetened Condensed Milk
   (NOT evaporated milk)
1 (16-ounce) container sour
   cream
½ cup frozen apple juice concentrate, thawed
2 eggs, beaten
1 teaspoon vanilla extract
2 medium all-purpose apples,
   pared and thinly sliced
½ cup apricot preserves
5 teaspoons water
1 teaspoon cornstarch

Continued next column

Glazed Apple Cream Tart

Preheat oven to 350°. In small mixer bowl, beat ½ cup margarine and sugar until fluffy. Stir in flour, oats and nuts; press firmly on bottom and halfway up side of lightly greased 9-inch spring-form pan. Bake 15 to 20 minutes or until golden. Meanwhile, in medium mixing bowl, combine sweetened condensed milk and sour cream; add juice concentrate, eggs and vanilla. Mix well. Pour into prepared crust. Bake 30 to 35 minutes or until center is set. Cool. In medium saucepan, melt remaining 2 tablespoons margarine. Add apples; cook and stir until tender. Arrange on top of tart. In small saucepan, combine preserves, water and cornstarch; cook and stir until preserves melt and mixture thickens slightly. Spoon over apples. Chill thoroughly. Refrigerate leftovers.

FLUFFY GRASSHOPPER PIE

Makes one 9-inch pie

2 cups finely crushed creme-
    filled chocolate sandwich
    cookies (about 20 cookies)
¼ cup margarine or butter, melted
1 (8-ounce) package cream
    cheese, softened
1 (14-ounce) can Eagle® Brand
    Sweetened Condensed Milk
    (NOT evaporated milk)
3 tablespoons ReaLemon®
    Lemon Juice from
    Concentrate
¼ cup green creme de menthe
¼ cup white creme de cacao
1 (4-ounce) container frozen
    non-dairy whipped topping,
    thawed *or* 1 cup (½ pint)
    whipping cream, stiffly
    whipped

Continued next column

Fluffy Grasshopper Pie

Combine crumbs and margarine; press firmly on bottom and up side of buttered 9-inch pie plate. Chill. Meanwhile, in large mixer bowl, beat cheese until fluffy; gradually beat in sweetened condensed milk until smooth. Stir in ReaLemon and liqueurs. Fold in whipped topping. Chill 20 minutes; pile into crust. Chill or freeze 4 hours or until set. Garnish as desired. Refrigerate or freeze leftovers.

CAKES & CHEESECAKES

FROM THE DESSERT MAKER

New York Style
Cheesecake (recipes page 34)

NEW YORK STYLE MARBLED CHEESECAKE

Makes one 9-inch cheesecake

⅓ cup margarine or butter, melted
1¼ cups graham cracker crumbs
¼ cup sugar
4 (8-ounce) packages cream cheese, softened
1 (14-ounce) can Eagle® Brand Sweetened Condensed Milk (NOT evaporated milk)
4 eggs
⅓ cup unsifted flour
1 tablespoon vanilla extract
2 to 4 (1-ounce) squares semi-sweet chocolate, melted

Preheat oven to 350°. Combine margarine, crumbs and sugar; press firmly on bottom of 9-inch springform pan. In large mixer bowl, beat cheese until fluffy. Gradually beat in sweetened condensed milk until smooth. Beat in eggs then flour and vanilla. Measure 1½ cups batter into medium mixing bowl. Add melted chocolate; mix well. Spoon half the yellow batter into prepared pan then half the chocolate batter. Repeat, ending with chocolate. With metal spatula, cut through batter to marble cake. Bake 1 hour or until lightly browned around edge. Cool to room temperature. Chill at least 6 hours. Garnish as desired. Refrigerate leftovers.

Tip: For best marbled effect, do not oversoften or overbeat cream cheese.

COOL AND MINTY PARTY CAKE

Makes one 9-inch cake

1 (14-ounce) can Eagle® Brand Sweetened Condensed Milk (NOT evaporated milk)
2 teaspoons peppermint extract
8 drops green food coloring
2 cups (1 pint) whipping cream, whipped (do not use non-dairy whipped topping)
1 (18½-ounce) package white cake mix
Green creme de menthe
1 (8-ounce) container frozen non-dairy whipped topping, thawed

In large mixing bowl, combine sweetened condensed milk, extract and food coloring. Fold in whipped cream. Pour into aluminum foil-lined 9-inch round layer cake pan; cover. Freeze at least 6 hours or overnight. Meanwhile, prepare and bake cake mix as package directs for two 9-inch round layers. Remove from pans; cool thoroughly. With table fork, poke holes in layers 1 inch apart halfway through each layer. Spoon small amounts of creme de menthe in holes. Place 1 cake layer on serving plate; top with ice cream layer then second cake layer. Trim ice cream layer to fit cake layers. Frost quickly with whipped topping. Return to freezer until ready to serve. Garnish as desired.

Tip: Cake can be made 1 week ahead and stored in freezer.

TEX-MEX SHEET CAKE

Makes one 15x10-inch cake

1¼ cups margarine or butter
½ cup unsweetened cocoa
2 tablespoons instant coffee
1 cup water
2 cups unsifted flour
1½ cups firmly packed light brown
    sugar
1 teaspoon baking soda
1 teaspoon ground cinnamon
½ teaspoon salt
1 (14-ounce) can Eagle® Brand
    Sweetened Condensed Milk
    (NOT evaporated milk)
2 eggs
1 teaspoon vanilla extract
1 cup confectioners' sugar
1 cup toasted slivered almonds
    or pecans

Preheat oven to 350°. In small sauce-pan, melt *1 cup* margarine; stir in *¼ cup* cocoa and *1 tablespoon* coffee, then water. Bring to a boil; remove from heat. In large mixer bowl, combine flour, brown sugar, baking soda, cinnamon and salt. Add cocoa mixture; mix well. Stir in *⅓ cup* sweetened condensed milk, eggs and vanilla. Pour into greased 15x10-inch jellyroll pan. Bake 15 minutes or until cake springs back when lightly touched. In small sauce-pan, melt remaining *¼ cup* margarine; stir in remaining *¼ cup* cocoa and *1 tablespoon* coffee. Add remaining sweetened condensed milk; stir in confectioners' sugar and nuts. Spread on warm cake.

CREAMY BAKED CHEESECAKE ▲

Makes one 9-inch cheesecake

⅓ cup margarine or butter, melted
1¼ cups graham cracker crumbs
¼ cup sugar
2 (8-ounce) packages cream
　cheese, softened
1 (14-ounce) can Eagle® Brand
　Sweetened Condensed Milk
　(NOT evaporated milk)
3 eggs
¼ cup ReaLemon® Lemon Juice
　from Concentrate
1 (8-ounce) container sour cream

Preheat oven to 300°. Combine
margarine, crumbs and sugar; press
firmly on bottom of 9-inch springform
pan. In large mixer bowl, beat cheese
until fluffy. Gradually beat in sweetened
condensed milk until smooth. Add eggs
and ReaLemon; mix well. Pour into
prepared pan. Bake 50 to 55 minutes or
until cake springs back when lightly
touched. Cool. Chill. Remove side of
pan. Spread sour cream on cheesecake.
Serve with Peach Melba Topping, page
40. Refrigerate leftovers.

New York Style Cheesecake: Omit
ReaLemon and sour cream. Preheat
oven to 350°. Beat 4 (8-ounce) packages cream cheese until fluffy. Gradually
add sweetened condensed milk; beat
until smooth. Add ⅓ cup unsifted flour,
4 eggs and 1 tablespoon vanilla extract;
mix well. Pour into prepared pan. Bake
1 hour or until lightly browned. Cool.
Chill. Garnish.

NO-BAKE CHOCOLATE CHEESECAKE

Makes one 9-inch cheesecake

⅓ cup margarine or butter, melted
1¼ cups graham cracker crumbs
¼ cup sugar
1 envelope unflavored gelatine
⅔ cup water
2 (8-ounce) packages cream
　cheese, softened
4 (1-ounce) squares semi-sweet
　chocolate, melted
1 (14-ounce) can Eagle® Brand
　Sweetened Condensed Milk
　(NOT evaporated milk)
1 teaspoon vanilla extract
1 cup (½ pint) whipping cream,
　whipped

Combine margarine, crumbs and sugar;
press firmly on bottom of 9-inch springform pan. In small saucepan, sprinkle
gelatine over water; let stand 1 minute.
Over low heat, stir until gelatine
dissolves; set aside. In large mixer
bowl, beat cheese and chocolate until
fluffy. Gradually beat in sweetened
condensed milk and vanilla until
smooth. Stir in gelatine mixture. Fold in
whipped cream. Pour into prepared
pan. Chill 3 hours or until set. Garnish
as desired. Refrigerate leftovers.

BUTTERSCOTCH CHEESECAKE

Makes one 9-inch cheesecake

- ⅓ cup margarine or butter, melted
- 1½ cups graham cracker crumbs
- ⅓ cup firmly packed brown sugar
- 1 (14-ounce) can Eagle® Brand Sweetened Condensed Milk (NOT evaporated milk)
- ¾ cup cold water
- 1 (3⅝-ounce) package butterscotch pudding and pie filling mix
- 3 (8-ounce) packages cream cheese, softened
- 3 eggs
- 1 teaspoon vanilla extract
  Whipped cream
  Crushed hard butterscotch candy

Continued next column

Butterscotch Cheesecake

Preheat oven to 375°. Combine margarine, crumbs and sugar; press firmly on bottom of 9-inch springform pan. In medium saucepan, combine sweetened condensed milk and water; mix well. Stir in pudding mix. Over medium heat, cook and stir until thickened and bubbly. In large mixer bowl, beat cheese until fluffy. Beat in eggs and vanilla then pudding mixture. Pour into prepared pan. Bake 50 minutes or until golden brown around edge (center will be soft). Cool to room temperature. Chill thoroughly. Garnish with whipped cream and crushed candy. Refrigerate leftovers.

BLACK FOREST TORTE

Makes one 9-inch cake

1 (18¼- or 18½-ounce) package
chocolate cake mix
1 (21-ounce) can cherry pie
filling, drained and chilled,
reserving ½ cup sauce
1 (6-ounce) package semi-sweet
chocolate chips
1 (14-ounce) can Eagle® Brand
Sweetened Condensed Milk
(NOT evaporated milk)
½ teaspoon almond extract

Preheat oven to 350°. Prepare and
bake cake mix as package directs for
two 9-inch round layers. Remove from
pans; cool thoroughly. In heavy saucepan, over medium heat, melt chips with
sweetened condensed milk. Cook and
stir until mixture thickens, about 10
minutes. Cool 20 minutes. Meanwhile,
combine cherries, reserved sauce and
extract. Place 1 cake layer on serving
plate, top side up. With sharp knife,
remove crust from top of cake layer to
within ½ inch of edge; top with half the
chocolate mixture then the cherries.
Top with second cake layer and remaining chocolate mixture. Garnish as
desired.

CHOCOLATE COCONUT PECAN TORTE

Makes one 8- or 9-inch cake

1 (18¼- or 18½-ounce) package
chocolate cake mix
1 (14-ounce) can Eagle® Brand
Sweetened Condensed Milk
(NOT evaporated milk)
3 egg yolks, beaten
½ cup margarine or butter
1 (3½-ounce) can flaked coconut
(1⅓ cups)
1 cup chopped pecans
1 teaspoon vanilla extract
2 cups frozen non-dairy whipped
topping, thawed or 1 cup
(½ pint) whipping cream,
whipped
Pecan halves, optional

Preheat oven to 350°. Prepare cake
mix as package directs. Pour batter into
three well-greased and floured 8- or
9-inch round layer cake pans. Bake 20
minutes or until wooden pick inserted
near center comes out clean. Remove
from pans; cool thoroughly. Meanwhile,
in heavy saucepan, combine sweetened
condensed milk, egg yolks and margarine. Over medium heat, cook and
stir until thickened or bubbly, about
10 minutes. Stir in coconut, pecans and
vanilla. Cool 10 minutes. With sharp
knife, remove crust from top of each
cake layer to within ½ inch of edge.
Spread equal portions of coconut
pecan mixture between layers and on
top to within ½ inch of edge. Frost side
and ½-inch rim on top of cake with
whipped topping. Garnish with pecan
halves if desired. Store cake in
refrigerator.

Pictured: Black Forest Torte, Chocolate
Coconut Pecan Torte.

CREAMY FRUIT 'N' NUT CHEESECAKE ▲

Makes one 9-inch cheesecake

⅓ cup margarine or butter, melted
1¼ cups graham cracker crumbs
¼ cup sugar
2 (8-ounce) packages cream cheese, softened
1 (14-ounce) can Eagle® Brand Sweetened Condensed Milk (NOT evaporated milk)
1 envelope unflavored gelatine
¼ cup ReaLemon® Lemon Juice from Concentrate
1⅓ cups (one-half 28-ounce jar) None Such® Ready-to-Use Mincemeat
½ cup chopped nuts
1 tablespoon grated lemon rind
1 cup (½ pint) whipping cream, whipped
Sour cream and additional nuts, optional

Continued next column

Creamy Fruit 'n' Nut Cheesecake

Combine margarine, crumbs and sugar; press firmly on bottom of 9-inch springform pan. In large mixer bowl, beat cheese until fluffy. Gradually beat in sweetened condensed milk until smooth. In small saucepan, sprinkle gelatine over ReaLemon; let stand 1 minute. Over low heat, stir until gelatine dissolves. Add to cheese mixture with mincemeat, nuts and rind; mix well. Fold in whipped cream; pour into prepared pan. Chill 3 hours or until set. Garnish with sour cream and additional nuts if desired. Refrigerate leftovers.

PEACH MELBA TOPPING

Reserve ⅔ cup syrup drained from 1 (10-ounce) package thawed frozen red raspberries. In small saucepan, combine reserved syrup, ¼ cup red currant jelly and 1 tablespoon cornstarch. Cook and stir until slightly thickened and glossy. Cool. Stir in raspberries. Drain 1 (16-ounce) can peach slices; arrange on cake. Top with sauce.

NO-BAKE PEACH CHEESECAKE

Makes one 9-inch cheesecake

⅓ cup margarine or butter, melted
1¼ cups graham cracker crumbs
¼ cup sugar
1 (29-ounce) can peach halves, drained, reserving syrup
1 envelope unflavored gelatine
2 (8-ounce) packages cream cheese, softened
1 (14-ounce) can Eagle® Brand Sweetened Condensed Milk (NOT evaporated milk)
2 tablespoons ReaLemon® Lemon Juice from Concentrate
1 (4-ounce) container frozen non-dairy whipped topping, thawed

Combine margarine, crumbs and sugar. Reserving 2 tablespoons for garnish, press remaining crumbs firmly on bottom of 9-inch springform pan or 13x9-inch baking pan. In small saucepan, sprinkle gelatine over ½ cup reserved syrup; let stand 1 minute. Over low heat, stir until gelatine dissolves. Slice 2 peach halves for garnish; reserve. In blender container, blend remaining peaches until smooth; combine with gelatine mixture and set aside. In large mixer bowl, beat cheese until fluffy; gradually beat in sweetened condensed milk until smooth. Stir in ReaLemon and peach mixture. Fold in whipped topping; turn into prepared pan. Chill 3 hours or until set. Garnish with peach slices. Refrigerate leftovers.

CHEESELESS "CHEESECAKE"

Makes 9 servings

4 eggs, separated
1 (14-ounce) can Eagle® Brand Sweetened Condensed Milk (NOT evaporated milk)
3 tablespoons ReaLemon® Lemon Juice from Concentrate
1½ teaspoons cornstarch
12 slices zwieback toast, crushed (about 1 cup)

Preheat oven to 350°. In medium mixing bowl, beat egg yolks. Add sweetened condensed milk, ReaLemon and cornstarch; mix well. In small mixer bowl, beat egg whites until stiff but not dry; fold into sweetened condensed milk mixture. Sprinkle half the zwieback crumbs into greased 9-inch square baking pan. Pour filling evenly over crumbs. Top with remaining crumbs. Bake 30 minutes or until wooden pick inserted near center comes out clean. Cool to room temperature. Chill thoroughly. Cut into squares to serve. Refrigerate leftovers.

LUSCIOUS BAKED CHOCOLATE CHEESECAKE

Makes one 9-inch cheesecake

1/3 cup margarine or butter, melted
1 1/4 cups graham cracker crumbs
1/4 cup sugar
3 (8-ounce) packages cream cheese, softened
1 (14-ounce) can Eagle® Brand Sweetened Condensed Milk (NOT evaporated milk)
1 (12-ounce) package semi-sweet chocolate chips *or* 8 (1-ounce) squares semi-sweet chocolate, melted
4 eggs
2 teaspoons vanilla extract

Preheat oven to 300°. Combine margarine, crumbs and sugar; press on bottom of 9-inch springform pan. In large mixer bowl, beat cheese until fluffy. Gradually beat in sweetened condensed milk until smooth. Add remaining ingredients; mix well. Pour into prepared pan. Bake 1 hour and 5 minutes or until cake springs back when lightly touched. Cool to room temperature. Chill thoroughly. Garnish as desired. Refrigerate leftovers.

PEANUT BUTTER FROSTING

Makes about 3 1/2 cups

1 (8-ounce) package cream cheese, softened
1 (14-ounce) can Eagle® Brand Sweetened Condensed Milk (NOT evaporated milk)
1 cup peanut butter

In small mixer bowl, beat cheese until fluffy. Gradually beat in sweetened condensed milk then peanut butter until smooth. Use to frost one (8- or 9-inch) two-layer cake *or* 4 dozen cupcakes *or* one (15x10-inch) sheét cake. Refrigerate leftovers.

CHOCOLATE CHIP CHEESECAKE

Makes one 9-inch cheesecake

1 1/2 cups finely crushed creme-filled chocolate sandwich cookies (about 18 cookies)
2 to 3 tablespoons margarine or butter, melted
3 (8-ounce) packages cream cheese, softened
1 (14-ounce) can Eagle® Brand Sweetened Condensed Milk (NOT evaporated milk)
3 eggs
2 teaspoons vanilla extract
1 cup mini chocolate chips
1 teaspoon flour

Preheat oven to 300°. Combine cookie crumbs and margarine; press firmly on bottom of 9-inch springform pan. In large mixer bowl, beat cheese until fluffy. Gradually beat in sweetened condensed milk until smooth. Add eggs and vanilla; mix well. In small bowl, toss *1/2 cup* chips with flour to coat; stir into cheese mixture. Pour into prepared pan. Sprinkle remaining *1/2 cup* chips evenly over top. Bake 1 hour or until cake springs back when lightly touched. Cool to room temperature. Chill thoroughly. Garnish as desired. Refrigerate leftovers.

Tip: For best distribution of chips through-out cheesecake, do not oversoften or overbeat cream cheese.

Pictured: Luscious Baked Chocolate Cheesecake, Chocolate Chip Cheesecake.

STRAWBERRY TUNNEL CREAM CAKE

Makes one 10-inch cake

1 (10-inch) prepared round angel food cake
2 (3-ounce) packages cream cheese, softened
1 (14-ounce) can Eagle® Brand Sweetened Condensed Milk (NOT evaporated milk)
⅓ cup ReaLemon® Lemon Juice from Concentrate
1 teaspoon almond extract
2 to 4 drops red food coloring, optional
1 cup chopped fresh strawberries
1 (12-ounce) container frozen non-dairy whipped topping, thawed (5¼ cups)
Additional fresh strawberries, optional

Continued next column

Strawberry Tunnel Cream Cake

Invert cake onto serving plate. Cut ½-inch slice crosswise from top of cake; set aside. With sharp knife, cut around cake 1 inch from center hole and 1 inch from outer edge, leaving cake walls 1-inch thick. Remove cake from center, leaving 1-inch thick base on bottom of cake. Reserve cake pieces. In large mixer bowl, beat cheese until fluffy. Gradually beat in sweetened condensed milk until smooth. Stir in ReaLemon, extract and food coloring if desired. Stir in reserved torn cake pieces and chopped strawberries. Fold in *1 cup* whipped topping. Fill cavity of cake with strawberry mixture; replace top slice of cake. Chill 3 hours or until set. Frost with remaining whipped topping; garnish with strawberries if desired. Store in refrigerator.

PEACH CREAM CAKE ▲

Makes 10 to 12 servings

1 (7-inch) prepared loaf angel
food cake, frozen
1 (14-ounce) can Eagle® Brand
Sweetened Condensed Milk
(NOT evaporated milk)
1 cup cold water
1 (3½-ounce) package instant
vanilla pudding and pie filling
mix
1 teaspoon almond extract
2 cups (1 pint) whipping cream,
whipped
4 cups sliced, pared fresh
peaches *or* 1 (20-ounce)
package frozen sliced
peaches, thawed

Cut cake into ¼-inch slices; arrange
half the slices on bottom of 13x9-inch
baking dish. In large mixer bowl,
combine sweetened condensed milk
and water; mix well. Add pudding mix;
beat until well blended. Chill 5 minutes.
Stir in extract; fold in whipped cream.
Pour half the cream mixture over cake
slices; arrange half the peach slices on
top. Repeat layering, ending with
peach slices. Chill 4 hours or until set.
Cut into squares to serve. Refrigerate
leftovers.

AMBROSIA COMPANY CAKE

Makes 12 to 15 servings

1 (18¼- or 18½-ounce) package
yellow or white cake mix
1 (14-ounce) can Eagle® Brand
Sweetened Condensed Milk
(NOT evaporated milk)
2 tablespoons frozen orange
juice concentrate, thawed
1 teaspoon grated orange rind
1 (4-ounce) container frozen
non-dairy whipped topping,
thawed
⅓ cup flaked coconut, toasted
Orange slices, optional

Preheat oven to 350°. Prepare and
bake cake as package directs for 13x9-
inch cake. Cool thoroughly. With table
knife handle, poke holes about 1 inch
apart in cake halfway through to bottom.
Combine sweetened condensed milk,
juice concentrate and rind; mix well.
Spoon small amounts of mixture into
each hole in cake; spread remaining
mixture evenly over top. Chill at least
1 hour. Spread whipped topping over
cake; garnish with coconut and orange
slices if desired. Store in refrigerator.

LEMON ANGEL ROLL

Makes 8 to 10 servings

1 (14½- or 16-ounce) package
    angel food cake mix
1 (14-ounce) can Eagle® Brand
    Sweetened Condensed Milk
    (NOT evaporated milk)
⅓ cup ReaLemon® Lemon Juice
    from Concentrate
2 teaspoons grated lemon rind
4 to 6 drops yellow food coloring,
    optional
1 (4-ounce) container frozen
    non-dairy whipped topping,
    thawed
½ cup flaked coconut, tinted
    yellow* if desired

Preheat oven to 350°. Line 15x10-inch
jellyroll pan with aluminum foil, extending foil 1 inch over ends of pan. Prepare
cake mix as package directs. Spread
batter evenly into prepared pan. Bake
30 minutes or until top springs back
when lightly touched. *Immediately* turn
onto towel sprinkled with confectioners'
sugar. Peel off foil; beginning at narrow
end, roll up cake with towel, jellyroll-
fashion. Cool thoroughly. Meanwhile, in
medium mixing bowl, combine sweetened condensed milk, ReaLemon, rind
and food coloring if desired; mix well.
Fold in whipped topping. Unroll cake;
trim edges. Spread with half the lemon
filling; reroll. Place on serving plate,
seam-side down; spread remaining
filling over roll. Garnish with coconut.
Chill thoroughly before serving. Store
in refrigerator.

*To tint coconut: Combine coconut,
½ teaspoon water and 2 drops yellow
food coloring in small plastic bag or
bowl; shake or mix well.

Continued next page

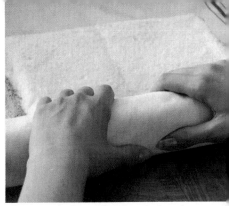

Lemon Angel Roll Variations:

Chocolate Pecan Filling

½ cup margarine or butter
1 (1-ounce) square unsweetened
   chocolate
1 (14-ounce) can Eagle® Brand
   Sweetened Condensed Milk
   (NOT evaporated milk)
1 (3½-ounce) can flaked coconut
   (1⅓ cups)
¾ cup finely chopped pecans
1 teaspoon vanilla extract

Prepare cake roll as above. In medium
saucepan, melt margarine and chocolate
with sweetened condensed milk. Over
medium heat, cook and stir until
mixture thickens, about 10 minutes.
Add coconut, nuts and vanilla. Spread
all filling on cake; proceed as above.
Sprinkle with confectioners' sugar.
Store covered at room temperature or
in refrigerator.

1. Invert cake *immediately* onto towel
sprinkled with confectioners' sugar.
Peel off foil. Roll up cake with towel;
cool.

Cranberry Filling

1 cup fresh *or* dry-pack frozen
   cranberries
½ cup sugar
¼ cup water
1 (3-ounce) package cream
   cheese, softened
1 (14-ounce) can Eagle® Brand
   Sweetened Condensed Milk
   (NOT evaporated milk)
¼ cup ReaLemon® Lemon Juice
   from Concentrate
Few drops red food coloring,
   optional

Prepare cake roll as above. In small
saucepan, combine cranberries, sugar
and water. Bring to a boil; reduce heat
and simmer uncovered 5 to 7 minutes.
Drain cranberries; puree in blender.
Cool. In small mixer bowl, beat cheese
until fluffy. Gradually beat in sweetened
condensed milk and ReaLemon until
smooth. Stir in cranberries and food
coloring if desired. Chill 1 hour.
Reserving 1½ cups mixture for outside,
spread remaining filling on cake;
proceed as above.

2. Unroll cooled cake. With serrated
knife, trim uneven crust edges.
Spread with filling.

3. Carefully roll cake and filling. Place
on serving plate, seam-side down.

LEMON PARTY CHEESECAKE

Makes 15 servings

1 (18¼- or 18½-ounce) package yellow cake mix*
4 eggs
¼ cup vegetable oil
2 (8-ounce) packages cream cheese, softened
1 (14-ounce) can Eagle® Brand Sweetened Condensed Milk (NOT evaporated milk)
¼ to ⅓ cup ReaLemon® Lemon Juice from Concentrate
2 teaspoons grated lemon rind
1 teaspoon vanilla extract

Preheat oven to 300°. Reserve ½ cup dry cake mix. In large mixer bowl, combine remaining cake mix, 1 egg and oil; mix well (mixture will be crumbly). Press firmly on bottom and 1½ inches up sides of greased 13x9-inch baking dish. In same bowl, beat cheese until fluffy. Gradually beat in sweetened condensed milk until smooth. Add remaining 3 eggs and reserved ½ cup cake mix; on medium speed, beat 1 minute. Stir in remaining ingredients. Pour into prepared pan. Bake 50 to 55 minutes or until center is firm. Cool to room temperature. Chill thoroughly. Cut into squares to serve. Garnish as desired. Refrigerate leftovers.

*If "pudding added" cake mix is used, decrease oil to 3 tablespoons.

Lemon Party Cheesecake

LEMON ORANGE SPICE CAKE

Makes one 8-inch cake

1 (18½-ounce) package spice cake mix
1 (14-ounce) can Eagle® Brand Sweetened Condensed Milk (NOT evaporated milk)
1 (6-ounce) can frozen orange juice concentrate, thawed
2 teaspoons grated orange rind
1 (4-ounce) container frozen non-dairy whipped topping, thawed

Preheat oven to 350°. Prepare and bake cake mix as package directs for two 8- or 9-inch round layers. Remove from pans; cool thoroughly. Split layers. In medium mixing bowl, combine sweetened condensed milk, juice concentrate and rind; mix well. Fold in whipped topping. Chill at least 1 hour. Use about ⅔ cup orange mixture between each layer; use remainder to frost top and side. Chill thoroughly. Store in refrigerator.

EVER-SO-EASY FRUITCAKE

Makes two 9x5-inch loaves

2½ cups unsifted flour
1 teaspoon baking soda
2 eggs, slightly beaten
1 (28-ounce) jar None Such®
Ready-to-Use Mincemeat
(Regular *or* Brandy and Rum)
1 (14-ounce) can Eagle® Brand
Sweetened Condensed Milk
(NOT evaporated milk)
2 cups (1 pound) mixed candied
fruit
1 cup coarsely chopped nuts

Preheat oven to 300°. Grease two 9x5-inch loaf pans. Combine flour and baking soda; set aside. In large bowl, combine remaining ingredients; blend in dry ingredients. Pour half the batter into each prepared pan. Bake 1 hour and 20 to 25 minutes or until wooden pick inserted near center comes out clean. Cool 15 minutes. Turn out of pan. Garnish as desired.

Continued next column

Ever-So-Easy Fruitcake Variations:

Fruitcake Bars: Grease 15x10-inch jellyroll pan; spread batter evenly in pan. Bake 40 to 45 minutes. Cool. Glaze if desired. Makes about 4 dozen bars.

Fruitcake-in-a-Can: Grease three 1-pound coffee cans; fill each can with about 2⅔ cups batter. Bake 1 hour and 20 to 25 minutes. *Or*, grease eight 10¾-ounce soup cans; fill each with 1 cup batter. Bake 50 to 55 minutes.

Bundt Fruitcake: Generously grease and flour 10-inch bundt pan; turn batter into pan. Bake 1 hour and 45 to 50 minutes.

Fruitcake Mini Loaves: Grease twelve 2½x4½-inch loaf pans. Fill each pan ⅔ full. Bake 35 to 40 minutes.

Tip: To substitute condensed mincemeat for ready-to-use mincemeat, crumble 2 (9-ounce) packages None Such® Condensed Mincemeat into small saucepan; add 1½ cups water. Boil briskly 1 minute. Cool. Proceed as above.

COOKIES & COOKIE BARS

FROM THE DESSERT MAKER

Pictured: Easy Peanut Butter Cookies, Choco-Coconut
Layer Bars, Peanut Blossoms (recipes page 52).

CHOCO-COCONUT LAYER BARS

Makes 24 bars

1/3 cup margarine or butter, melted
3/4 cup unsifted flour
1/2 cup sugar
2 tablespoons unsweetened
  cocoa
1 egg
1 (14-ounce) can Eagle® Brand
  Sweetened Condensed Milk
  (NOT evaporated milk)
1 (3 1/2-ounce) can flaked coconut
  (1 1/3 cups)
Flavor Variations*
1 (6-ounce) package semi-sweet
  chocolate chips

Preheat oven to 350° (325° for glass
dish). In medium mixing bowl, combine
margarine, flour, sugar, cocoa and egg;
mix well. Spread evenly into lightly
greased 9-inch square baking pan. In
small bowl, combine 3/4 cup sweetened
condensed milk, coconut and desired
flavor variation; spread over chocolate
layer. Bake 20 minutes or until lightly
browned around edges. In heavy
saucepan, over low heat, melt chips
with remaining sweetened condensed
milk. Remove from heat; spread evenly
over coconut layer. Cool. Chill thoroughly. Cut into bars. Store loosely
covered at room temperature.

*Flavor Variations:

Almond

1 cup chopped slivered almonds
1/2 teaspoon almond extract

Mint

1/2 teaspoon peppermint extract
4 drops green food coloring,
  optional

Cherry

2 (6-ounce) jars maraschino
  cherries, chopped and well
  drained on paper towels

EASY PEANUT BUTTER COOKIES

Makes about 5 dozen

1 (14-ounce) can Eagle® Brand
  Sweetened Condensed Milk
  (NOT evaporated milk)
3/4 cup peanut butter
2 cups biscuit baking mix
1 teaspoon vanilla extract
Granulated sugar

Preheat oven to 375°. In large mixer
bowl, beat sweetened condensed milk
and peanut butter until smooth. Add
biscuit mix and vanilla; mix well. Shape
into 1-inch balls. Roll in sugar. Place
2 inches apart on ungreased baking
sheets. Flatten with fork. Bake 6 to
8 minutes or until *lightly* browned (do
not overbake). Cool. Store tightly
covered at room temperature.

Peanut Blossoms: Shape as above; *do
not flatten.* Bake as above. Press milk
chocolate candy kiss in center of each
ball immediately after baking.

Peanut Butter & Jelly Gems: Press
thumb in center of each ball of dough;
fill with jelly, jam or preserves. Bake as
above.

Any-Way-You-Like'm Cookies: Stir
1 cup semi-sweet chocolate chips *or*
chopped peanuts *or* raisins *or* flaked
coconut into dough. Proceed as above.

COCONUT MACAROONS

Makes about 4 dozen

**2 (7-ounce) packages *flaked*
 coconut (5⅓ cups)
1 (14-ounce) can Eagle® Brand
 Sweetened Condensed Milk
 (NOT evaporated milk)
2 teaspoons vanilla extract
1½ teaspoons almond extract**

Preheat oven to 350°. In large mixing
bowl, combine coconut, sweetened
condensed milk and extracts; mix well.
Drop by rounded teaspoonfuls onto
aluminum foil-lined and *generously
greased* baking sheets; garnish as
desired. Bake 8 to 10 minutes or until
lightly browned around edges. *Immediately* remove from baking sheets
(macaroons will stick if allowed to cool).
Store loosely covered at room
temperature.

Chocolate: Omit almond extract. Add
4 (1-ounce) squares unsweetened
chocolate, melted. Proceed as above.

Chocolate Chip: Omit almond extract.
Add 1 cup mini chocolate chips.
Proceed as above.

Cherry Nut: Omit almond extract. Add
1 cup chopped nuts and 2 tablespoons
maraschino cherry syrup. Press
maraschino cherry half into center of
each macaroon before baking.

Rum Raisin: Omit almond extract. Add
1 cup raisins and 1 teaspoon rum
flavoring. Proceed as above.

Almond Brickle: Add ½ cup almond
brickle chips. Proceed as above. Bake
10 to 12 minutes. Cool 3 minutes;
remove from baking sheets.

Maple Walnut: Omit almond extract.
Add ½ cup finely chopped walnuts and
½ teaspoon maple flavoring. Proceed
as above.

Nutty Oat: Omit almond extract. Add
1 cup oats and 1 cup chopped nuts.
Proceed as above.

Tip: To reduce cost, omit 1 (7-ounce)
package coconut and substitute 2 cups
fresh bread crumbs (4 slices bread).

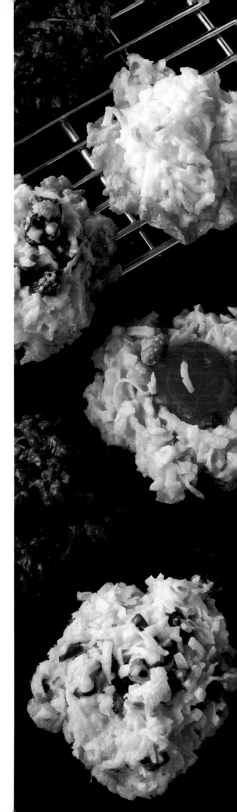

PECAN PIE BARS

Makes 36 bars

2 cups unsifted flour
½ cup confectioners' sugar
1 cup cold margarine or butter
1 (14-ounce) can Eagle® Brand
Sweetened Condensed Milk
(NOT evaporated milk)
1 egg
1 teaspoon vanilla extract
1 (6-ounce) package almond
brickle chips
1 cup chopped pecans

Preheat oven to 350° (325° for glass dish). In medium mixing bowl, combine flour and sugar; cut in margarine until mixture resembles coarse corn meal. Press firmly on bottom of 13x9-inch baking pan. Bake 15 minutes. Meanwhile, in medium mixing bowl, beat sweetened condensed milk, egg and vanilla. Stir in chips and pecans. Spread evenly over prepared crust. Bake 25 minutes or until golden brown. Cool. Chill thoroughly. Cut into bars. Store covered in refrigerator.

TRIPLE LAYER COOKIE BARS

Makes 36 bars

½ cup margarine or butter
1½ cups graham cracker crumbs
1 (7-ounce) package flaked
coconut (2⅔ cups)
1 (14-ounce) can Eagle® Brand
Sweetened Condensed Milk
(NOT evaporated milk)
1 (12-ounce) package semi-
sweet chocolate chips
½ cup creamy peanut butter

Preheat oven to 350° (325° for glass dish). In 13x9-inch baking pan, melt margarine in oven. Sprinkle crumbs evenly over margarine. Top evenly with coconut then sweetened condensed milk. Bake 25 minutes or until lightly browned. In small saucepan, over low heat, melt chips with peanut butter. Spread evenly over hot coconut layer. Cool 30 minutes. Chill thoroughly. Cut into bars. Store loosely covered at room temperature.

MINI FRUITCAKE MORSELS

Makes about 7 dozen

½ cup unsifted flour
1 teaspoon baking soda
1 (28-ounce) jar None Such®
  Ready-to-Use Mincemeat
1 (14-ounce) can Eagle® Brand
  Sweetened Condensed Milk
  (NOT evaporated milk)
2 cups graham cracker crumbs
1 cup chopped nuts
3 eggs, beaten
  Red and green candied
  cherries, halved

Preheat oven to 300°. In large mixing
bowl, combine flour and baking soda.
Add remaining ingredients except
cherries; mix well. Line 1¾-inch muffin
cups with paper liners or grease lightly.
Spoon 1 level measuring tablespoon
batter into each cup. Top each with
cherry half. Bake 25 to 30 minutes or
until wooden pick inserted near center
comes out clean. Cool. Store loosely
covered at room temperature.

CRUNCH BARS

Makes 36 bars

5 cups bite-size crispy rice or
  wheat squares
½ cup margarine or butter
1 cup butterscotch or peanut
  butter flavored chips
1 (3½-ounce) can flaked coconut
  (1⅓ cups)
1 (14-ounce) can Eagle® Brand
  Sweetened Condensed Milk
  (NOT evaporated milk)
1 cup chopped pecans

Preheat oven to 350° (325° for glass
dish). Coarsely crush 3 cups cereal. In
13x9-inch baking pan, melt margarine
in oven. Sprinkle crushed cereal over
margarine; top evenly with chips,
coconut, sweetened condensed milk,
nuts and 2 cups uncrushed cereal.
Press down firmly. Bake 25 to 30
minutes or until lightly browned. Cool
thoroughly. Cut into bars. Store loosely
covered at room temperature.

CASHEW PEANUT BUTTER BARS

Makes 36 bars

1 cup unsifted flour
¼ cup firmly packed brown sugar
½ teaspoon baking powder
¼ teaspoon baking soda
½ cup cold margarine or butter, cut into small pieces
1 tablespoon vanilla extract
3 cups Campfire® Miniature Marshmallows
1 (14-ounce) can Eagle® Brand Sweetened Condensed Milk (NOT evaporated milk)
1 cup peanut butter flavored chips or ½ cup creamy peanut butter
1 (3-ounce) can chow mein noodles
1 cup coarsely chopped cashews or peanuts

Preheat oven to 350°. In medium mixing bowl, combine flour, sugar, baking powder and baking soda. Cut in margarine and *1 teaspoon* vanilla until mixture resembles coarse corn meal. Press firmly on bottom of ungreased 13x9-inch baking pan. Bake 15 minutes or until lightly browned. Top evenly with marshmallows; bake 2 minutes longer or until marshmallows begin to puff. Remove from oven; cool. Meanwhile, in heavy saucepan, over medium heat, combine sweetened condensed milk and peanut butter chips; cook and stir until slightly thickened, 6 to 8 minutes. Remove from heat; stir in remaining ingredients. Spread evenly over marshmallows. Chill thoroughly. Cut into bars. Store loosely covered at room temperature.

DOUBLE CHOCOLATE CHERRY COOKIES

Makes about 10 dozen

1¼ cups margarine or butter, softened
1¾ cups sugar
2 eggs
1 tablespoon vanilla extract
3½ cups unsifted flour
¾ cup unsweetened cocoa
½ teaspoon baking powder
½ teaspoon baking soda
¼ teaspoon salt
2 (6-ounce) jars maraschino cherries, well drained and halved (about 60 cherries)
1 (6-ounce) package semi-sweet chocolate chips
1 (14-ounce) can Eagle® Brand Sweetened Condensed Milk (NOT evaporated milk)

Continued next column

Double Chocolate Cherry Cookies

Preheat oven to 350°. In large mixer bowl, beat margarine and sugar until fluffy; add eggs and vanilla. Mix well. Combine dry ingredients; stir into margarine mixture (dough will be stiff). Shape into 1-inch balls. Place 1 inch apart on ungreased baking sheets. Press cherry half into center of each cookie. Bake 8 to 10 minutes. Cool. In heavy saucepan, over medium heat, melt chips with sweetened condensed milk; continue cooking about 3 minutes or until mixture thickens. Frost each cookie, covering cherry. Store loosely covered at room temperature.

Double Chocolate Pecan Cookies:
Prepare cookies as directed omitting cherries; flatten. Bake as directed and frost tops. Garnish each cookie with pecan half.

APPLESAUCE FRUITCAKE BARS ▲

Makes 48 bars

1 (14-ounce) can Eagle® Brand
  Sweetened Condensed Milk
  (NOT evaporated milk)
2 eggs
¼ cup margarine or butter, melted
2 teaspoons vanilla extract
3 cups biscuit baking mix
1 (15-ounce) jar applesauce
1 cup chopped dates
1 (6-ounce) container green
  candied cherries, chopped
1 (6-ounce) container red
  candied cherries, chopped
1 cup chopped nuts
1 cup raisins
  Confectioners' sugar

Preheat oven to 325°. In large mixer bowl, beat sweetened condensed milk, eggs, margarine and vanilla. Stir in remaining ingredients except confectioners' sugar. Spread evenly into well-greased and floured 15x10-inch jellyroll pan. Bake 35 to 40 minutes or until wooden pick inserted in center comes out clean. Cool thoroughly. Sprinkle with confectioners' sugar. Cut into bars. Store tightly covered at room temperature.

QUICK FRUIT SNACK MUNCHIES

Makes about 5 dozen

1 (14-ounce) can Eagle® Brand
  Sweetened Condensed Milk
  (NOT evaporated milk)
2 cups finely chopped dried
  apricots or dates
¾ cup finely chopped nuts
1 teaspoon vanilla extract
1 (12-ounce) package butter- or
  cheese-flavored crackers

In heavy saucepan, over medium heat, combine sweetened condensed milk and apricots; cook and stir until thickened, about 8 minutes. Remove from heat; stir in nuts and vanilla. Spoon about 1 teaspoon mixture on cracker; top with another cracker. Repeat. Store covered at room temperature.

MICROWAVE: In 1-quart glass measure, combine sweetened condensed milk and apricots. Microwave on ½ power (medium) 5 to 6 minutes, stirring after 3 minutes. Stir in nuts and vanilla. Proceed as above.

CHOCOLATE PEANUT BUTTER CHIP COOKIES ▶

Makes about 4 dozen

- 8 (1-ounce) squares semi-sweet chocolate
- 3 tablespoons margarine or butter
- 1 (14-ounce) can Eagle® Brand Sweetened Condensed Milk (NOT evaporated milk)
- 2 cups biscuit baking mix
- 1 teaspoon vanilla extract
- 1 cup peanut butter flavored chips

Preheat oven to 350°. In large saucepan, over low heat, melt chocolate and margarine with sweetened condensed milk; remove from heat. Add biscuit mix and vanilla; with mixer, beat until smooth and well blended. Cool to room temperature. Stir in chips. Shape into 1¼-inch balls. Place 2 inches apart on ungreased baking sheets. Bake 6 to 8 minutes or until tops are slightly crusted. Cool. Store tightly covered at room temperature.

QUICK NO-BAKE BROWNIES

Makes 24 brownies

- 1 cup finely chopped nuts
- 2 (1-ounce) squares un-sweetened chocolate
- 1 (14-ounce) can Eagle® Brand Sweetened Condensed Milk (NOT evaporated milk)
- 2 to 2½ cups vanilla wafer crumbs (about 48 to 60 wafers)

In buttered 9-inch square pan, sprinkle ¼ *cup* nuts. In heavy saucepan, over low heat, melt chocolate with sweetened condensed milk. Cook and stir until mixture thickens, about 10 minutes. Remove from heat; stir in crumbs and ½ *cup* nuts. Spread evenly into prepared pan. Top with remaining ¼ *cup* nuts. Chill 4 hours or until firm. Cut into squares. Store loosely covered at room temperature.

MAGIC COOKIE BARS ▲

Makes 36 bars

½ cup margarine or butter
1½ cups graham cracker *or* other
    crumbs*
1 (14-ounce) can Eagle® Brand
    Sweetened Condensed Milk
    (NOT evaporated milk)
1 cup semi-sweet chocolate
    chips *or* other toppings**
1 (3½-ounce) can flaked coconut
    (1⅓ cups)
1 cup chopped nuts***

Preheat oven to 350° (325° for glass
dish). In 13x9-inch baking pan, melt
margarine in oven. Sprinkle crumbs
over margarine; pour sweetened
condensed milk evenly over crumbs.
Sprinkle with chips then coconut and
nuts; press down firmly. Bake 25 to 30
minutes or until lightly browned. Cool.
Chill thoroughly if desired. Cut into
bars. Store loosely covered at room
temperature.

Continued next column

Magic Cookie Bars

*Crumbs

Vanilla wafer
Chocolate wafer
Gingersnap cookie
Quick-cooking oats
Wheat germ

**Toppings

Peanut butter flavored chips
Butterscotch flavored chips
Plain multi-colored candy-coated
    chocolate pieces
Raisins
Chopped dried apricots
Almond brickle chips
Banana chips
Chopped candied cherries
Small gumdrop candies
Miniature marshmallows

***Nuts

Walnuts
Pecans
Almonds
Peanuts
Cashews
Macadamia

Continued next page

Magic Cookie Bars

Flavor Variations:

Mint: Combine ½ teaspoon peppermint extract and 4 drops green food coloring if desired with sweetened condensed milk. Proceed as above.

Mocha: Add 1 tablespoon instant coffee and 1 tablespoon chocolate flavored syrup with sweetened condensed milk. Proceed as above.

Peanut Butter: Combine ⅓ cup peanut butter with sweetened condensed milk. Proceed as above.

Maple: Combine ½ to 1 teaspoon maple flavoring with sweetened condensed milk. Proceed as above.

BANANA COOKIE BARS

Makes 36 bars

½ cup margarine or butter
1½ cups graham cracker crumbs
1 (14-ounce) can Eagle® Brand Sweetened Condensed Milk (NOT evaporated milk)
2 medium bananas, mashed (about 1 cup)
1 (6-ounce) package semi-sweet chocolate chips
1 (3½-ounce) can flaked coconut (1⅓ cups)
1 cup chopped nuts

Preheat oven to 350° (325° for glass dish). In 13x9-inch baking pan, melt margarine in oven. Sprinkle crumbs over margarine. In small bowl, combine sweetened condensed milk and bananas; pour evenly over crumbs. Top with remaining ingredients; press down firmly. Bake 25 to 30 minutes or until lightly browned. Cool. Chill thoroughly. Cut into bars. Store covered in refrigerator.

TOFFEE BARS

Makes 36 bars

½ cup margarine or butter
1 cup oats
½ cup firmly packed brown sugar
½ cup unsifted flour
½ cup finely chopped walnuts
¼ teaspoon baking soda
1 (14-ounce) can Eagle® Brand
  Sweetened Condensed Milk
  (NOT evaporated milk)
2 teaspoons vanilla extract
1 (6-ounce) package semi-sweet
  chocolate chips

Preheat oven to 350°. In medium
saucepan, melt 6 *tablespoons* margarine; stir in oats, sugar, flour, nuts and
baking soda. Press firmly on bottom of
greased 13x9-inch baking pan; bake 10
to 15 minutes or until lightly browned.
Meanwhile, in medium saucepan,
combine remaining 2 *tablespoons*
margarine and sweetened condensed
milk. Over medium heat, cook and stir
until mixture thickens slightly, about 15
minutes. Remove from heat; stir in
vanilla. Pour over crust. Return to oven;
bake 10 to 15 minutes longer or until
golden brown. Remove from oven;
immediately sprinkle chips on top. Let
stand 1 minute; spread while still warm.
Cool to room temperature; chill
thoroughly. Cut into bars. Store tightly
covered at room temperature.

MACAROON ALMOND CRUMB BARS

Makes 36 bars

1 (18¼- or 18½-ounce) package
  chocolate cake mix
¼ cup vegetable oil
2 eggs
1 (14-ounce) can Eagle® Brand
  Sweetened Condensed Milk
  (NOT evaporated milk)
½ to 1 teaspoon almond extract
1½ cups coconut macaroon
  crumbs (about 8 macaroons)
1 cup chopped slivered almonds

Continued next column

Macaroon Almond Crumb Bars

Preheat oven to 350° (325° for glass
dish). In large mixer bowl, combine
cake mix, oil and *1 egg*. Beat on
medium speed until crumbly. Press
firmly on bottom of greased 13x9-inch
baking pan. In medium mixing bowl,
combine sweetened condensed milk,
remaining egg and extract; mix well.
Add *1 cup* macaroon crumbs and
almonds. Spread evenly over prepared
crust. Sprinkle with remaining *½ cup*
crumbs. Bake 30 to 35 minutes or until
lightly browned. Cool thoroughly. Cut
into bars. Store loosely covered at
room temperature.

DOUBLE CHOCOLATE FANTASY BARS

Makes 36 bars

1 (18¼- or 18½-ounce) package
  chocolate cake mix
¼ cup vegetable oil
1 egg
1 cup chopped nuts
1 (14-ounce) can Eagle® Brand
  Sweetened Condensed Milk
  (NOT evaporated milk)
1 (6-ounce) package semi-sweet
  chocolate chips
1 teaspoon vanilla extract
  Dash salt

Preheat oven to 350°. In large mixer
bowl, combine cake mix, oil and egg;
beat on medium speed until crumbly.
Stir in nuts. Reserving 1½ cups crumb
mixture, press remainder on bottom of
greased 13x9-inch baking pan. In small
saucepan, combine remaining ingredients. Over medium heat, cook and
stir until chips melt. Pour evenly over
prepared crust. Sprinkle reserved
crumb mixture evenly over top. Bake
25 to 30 minutes or until bubbly. Cool
thoroughly. Cut into bars. Store loosely
covered at room temperature.

Pictured Top to Bottom: Double Chocolate
Fantasy Bars, Macaroon Almond Crumb
Bars, Toffee Bars.

GERMAN CHOCOLATE SNACKIN' BARS ▲

Makes 36 bars

1 (4-ounce) package sweet
　cooking chocolate
¼ cup margarine or butter
1 (14-ounce) can Eagle® Brand
　Sweetened Condensed Milk
　(NOT evaporated milk)
2 eggs
½ cup biscuit baking mix
1 teaspoon vanilla extract
1 (7-ounce) package flaked
　coconut (2⅔ cups)
1 cup chopped pecans

Preheat oven to 325°. In medium
saucepan, over low heat, melt chocolate with margarine. Remove from heat;
stir in ½ cup sweetened condensed
milk, eggs, biscuit mix and vanilla.
Spread evenly into greased 13x9-inch
baking dish. In medium bowl, combine
remaining sweetened condensed milk
and coconut. Spoon in small amounts
evenly over chocolate mixture. Sprinkle
nuts over top; press down firmly. Bake
25 minutes or until wooden pick
inserted near center comes out clean.
Cool thoroughly. Cut into bars. Store
loosely covered at room temperature.

MILK CHOCOLATE BROWNIES

Makes 40 brownies

1 (12-ounce) package semi-
　sweet chocolate chips
¼ cup margarine or butter
2 cups biscuit baking mix
1 (14-ounce) can Eagle® Brand
　Sweetened Condensed Milk
　(NOT evaporated milk)
1 egg, beaten
1 teaspoon vanilla extract
1 cup chopped walnuts
　Confectioners' sugar

Preheat oven to 350°. In large saucepan, over low heat, melt *1 cup* chips
with margarine; remove from heat. Add
biscuit mix, sweetened condensed
milk, egg and vanilla. Stir in nuts and
remaining chips. Turn into well-greased
13x9-inch baking pan. Bake 20 to 25
minutes or until brownies begin to pull
away from side of pan. Cool. Sprinkle
with confectioners' sugar. Cut into
squares. Store tightly covered at room
temperature.

BUTTERSCOTCH CHEESECAKE BARS

Makes 36 bars

1 (12-ounce) package butterscotch flavored chips
⅓ cup margarine or butter
2 cups graham cracker crumbs
1 cup chopped nuts
1 (8-ounce) package cream
cheese, softened
1 (14-ounce) can Eagle® Brand
Sweetened Condensed Milk
(NOT evaporated milk)
1 egg
1 teaspoon vanilla extract

Preheat oven to 350° (325° for glass
dish). In medium saucepan, melt chips
and margarine; stir in crumbs and nuts.
Press half the mixture firmly on bottom
of greased 13x9-inch baking pan. In
large mixer bowl, beat cheese until
fluffy; gradually beat in sweetened
condensed milk then egg and vanilla.
Mix well. Pour into prepared pan; top
evenly with remaining crumb mixture.
Bake 25 to 30 minutes or until wooden
pick inserted near center comes out
clean. Cool. Chill thoroughly. Cut into
bars. Store covered in refrigerator.

NO-BAKE PEANUTTY CHOCOLATE DROPS

Makes about 5 dozen

½ cup margarine or butter
⅓ cup unsweetened cocoa
1 (14-ounce) can Eagle® Brand
Sweetened Condensed Milk
(NOT evaporated milk)
2½ cups quick-cooking oats
1 cup chopped peanuts
½ cup peanut butter

In medium saucepan, melt margarine;
stir in cocoa. Bring mixture to a boil.
Remove from heat; stir in remaining
ingredients. Drop by teaspoonfuls onto
waxed paper-lined baking sheets; chill
2 hours or until set. Store loosely
covered in refrigerator.

MAKE-AHEAD S'MORES

Makes 64 servings

1 (8-ounce) package semi-sweet
chocolate squares
1 (14-ounce) can Eagle® Brand
Sweetened Condensed Milk
(NOT evaporated milk)
1 teaspoon vanilla extract
2 cups Campfire® Miniature
Marshmallows
32 (4¾x2⅛-inch) whole graham
crackers

In heavy saucepan, over low heat, melt
chocolate. Add sweetened condensed
milk and vanilla; cook and stir until
smooth. Making 1 sandwich at a time,
spread 1 tablespoon chocolate mixture
on each of 2 whole graham crackers;
sprinkle 1 with marshmallows and
gently press second graham cracker
chocolate-side down on top. Repeat
with remaining ingredients. Carefully
break each sandwich in half before
serving. Wrap with plastic wrap; store at
room temperature.

MICROWAVE: In 1-quart glass measure,
combine chocolate, sweetened condensed milk and vanilla. Microwave on
full power (high) 2½ minutes. Stir until
chocolate melts and mixture is smooth.
Proceed as above.

Make-Ahead S'Mores

CHOCOLATE MINT BARS

Makes 48 bars

1 (6-ounce) package semi-sweet chocolate chips
1 (14-ounce) can Eagle® Brand Sweetened Condensed Milk (NOT evaporated milk)
¾ cup plus 2 tablespoons margarine or butter
½ teaspoon peppermint extract
1¼ cups firmly packed light brown sugar
1 egg
1½ cups unsifted flour
1½ cups quick-cooking oats
¾ cup chopped nuts
⅓ cup crushed hard peppermint candy, optional

Preheat oven to 350°. In heavy saucepan, over low heat, melt chips with sweetened condensed milk and *2 tablespoons* margarine; remove from heat. Add extract; set aside. In large mixer bowl, beat remaining *¾ cup* margarine and sugar until fluffy; beat in egg. Add flour and oats; mix well. With floured hands, press two-thirds oat mixture into greased 15x10-inch jellyroll pan; spread chocolate mixture evenly on top. Add nuts to remaining oat mixture; crumble evenly over chocolate. Sprinkle with peppermint candy if desired. Bake 15 to 18 minutes or until edges are lightly browned. Cool thoroughly. Cut into bars. Store loosely covered at room temperature.

Pictured Top to Bottom: Double Peanut-Choco Bars, Chocolate Mint Bars, Layered Lemon Crumb Bars.

LAYERED LEMON CRUMB BARS

Makes 36 bars

1 (14-ounce) can Eagle® Brand
  Sweetened Condensed Milk
  (NOT evaporated milk)
½ cup ReaLemon® Lemon Juice
  from Concentrate
1 teaspoon grated lemon rind
⅔ cup margarine or butter,
  softened
1 cup firmly packed light brown
  sugar
1½ cups unsifted flour
1 cup oats
1 teaspoon baking powder
½ teaspoon salt
½ teaspoon ground cinnamon
½ teaspoon ground nutmeg

Preheat oven to 350° (325° for glass dish). In small mixing bowl, combine sweetened condensed milk, ReaLemon and rind; set aside. In large mixer bowl, beat margarine and sugar until fluffy; add flour, oats, baking powder and salt. Mix until crumbly. Spread half the oat mixture into lightly greased 13x9-inch baking pan. Press down firmly; spread lemon mixture evenly over crust. Stir spices into remaining crumb mixture; sprinkle evenly over lemon layer. Bake 20 to 25 minutes or until lightly browned. Chill thoroughly. Cut into bars. Store covered in refrigerator.

DOUBLE PEANUT-CHOCO BARS

Makes 36 bars

1 (18¼- or 18½-ounce) package
  white cake mix
½ cup plus ⅓ cup peanut butter
1 egg
1 (14-ounce) can Eagle® Brand
  Sweetened Condensed Milk
  (NOT evaporated milk)
1 (6-ounce) package semi-sweet
  chocolate chips
¾ cup Spanish peanuts

Continued next column

Double Peanut-Choco Bars

Preheat oven to 350° (325° for glass dish). In large mixer bowl, combine cake mix, ½ cup peanut butter and egg; beat on low speed until crumbly. Press firmly on bottom of greased 13x9-inch baking pan. In medium mixing bowl, combine sweetened condensed milk and remaining ⅓ cup peanut butter; mix well. Spread evenly over prepared crust. Top with chips and peanuts. Bake 30 to 35 minutes or until lightly browned. Cool thoroughly. Cut into bars. Store loosely covered at room temperature.

CHOCOLATE ALMOND BARS

Makes 24 bars

1 cup slivered almonds, toasted
  and chopped
¼ cup margarine or butter, melted
1 (14-ounce) can Eagle® Brand
  Sweetened Condensed Milk
  (NOT evaporated milk)
1¼ cups graham cracker crumbs
½ teaspoon almond extract
½ teaspoon ground cinnamon,
  optional
1 (6-ounce) package semi-sweet
  chocolate chips

Preheat oven to 350°. In large mixing bowl, combine all ingredients except ½ cup chocolate chips; mix well. Spread evenly into greased 12x7-inch baking dish. Bake 20 minutes or until golden brown. Remove from oven; immediately sprinkle remaining ½ cup chips over top. Let stand 1 minute; spread while still warm. Cool thoroughly. Cut into bars. Store loosely covered at room temperature.

GRANOLA BARS

Makes 48 bars

3 cups oats
1 cup peanuts
1 cup raisins
1 cup sunflower meats
1½ teaspoons ground cinnamon
1 (14-ounce) can Eagle® Brand Sweetened Condensed Milk (NOT evaporated milk)
½ cup margarine or butter, melted

Preheat oven to 325°. Line 15x10-inch jellyroll pan with aluminum foil; grease. In large mixing bowl, combine all ingredients; mix well. Press evenly into prepared pan. Bake 25 to 30 minutes or until golden brown. Cool slightly; remove from pan and peel off foil. Cut into bars. Store loosely covered at room temperature.

PEANUTTY OAT BARS

Makes 36 bars

¼ cup margarine or butter
1½ cups quick-cooking oats
1 (3½-ounce) can flaked coconut (1⅓ cups)
1 (14-ounce) can Eagle® Brand Sweetened Condensed Milk (NOT evaporated milk)
1 cup peanut butter flavored chips
1 cup chopped nuts

Preheat oven to 350° (325° for glass dish). In 13x9-inch baking pan, melt margarine in oven. Sprinkle oats over margarine then coconut. Pour sweetened condensed milk evenly over top. Top evenly with chips then nuts; press down firmly. Bake 25 to 30 minutes or until lightly browned. Cool thoroughly. Cut into bars. Store loosely covered at room temperature.

VERSATILE CUT-OUT COOKIES

Makes about 6½ dozen

3 cups unsifted flour
1 tablespoon baking powder
½ teaspoon salt
1 (14-ounce) can Eagle® Brand Sweetened Condensed Milk (NOT evaporated milk)
¾ cup margarine or butter, softened
2 eggs
2 teaspoons vanilla or 1½ teaspoons almond or lemon extract
Ready-to-spread frosting

Preheat oven to 350°. Combine flour, baking powder and salt; set aside. In large mixer bowl, beat sweetened condensed milk, margarine, eggs and vanilla until well blended. Add dry ingredients; mix well. On floured surface, lightly knead dough to form a smooth ball. Divide into thirds. On well-floured surface, roll out each portion to ⅛-inch thickness. Cut with floured cookie cutter. Place 1 inch apart on greased baking sheets. Bake 7 to 9 minutes or until lightly browned around edges. Cool thoroughly. Frost and decorate as desired with ready-to-spread frosting. Store loosely covered at room temperature.

Sandwich Cookies: Use 2½-inch cookie cutter. Bake as directed. Sandwich 2 cookies together with ready-to-spread frosting. Sprinkle with sugar if desired. (Makes about 3 dozen)

Versatile Cut-Out Cookies.

Pictured: Strawberries & Cream Dessert
(recipe page 72).

CLASSIC DESSERTS

STRAWBERRIES & CREAM DESSERT

Makes 10 to 12 servings

1 (14-ounce) can Eagle® Brand Sweetened Condensed Milk (NOT evaporated milk)
1½ cups cold water
1 (3½-ounce) package instant vanilla pudding and pie filling mix
2 cups (1 pint) whipping cream, whipped
1 (12-ounce) prepared loaf pound cake, cut into cubes (about 6 cups)
4 cups sliced fresh strawberries
½ cup strawberry preserves
Additional fresh strawberries
Toasted slivered almonds

In large mixing bowl, combine sweetened condensed milk and water; mix well. Add pudding mix; beat until well blended. Chill 5 minutes. Fold in whipped cream. Spoon *2 cups* pudding mixture into 4-quart round glass serving bowl; top with half the cake cubes, half the strawberries, half the preserves and half the remaining pudding mixture. Repeat layering, ending with pudding mixture. Garnish with additional strawberries and almonds. Chill 4 hours or until set. Refrigerate leftovers.

CREAMY LEMON FROSTING

Makes about 2½ cups

1 (8-ounce) package cream cheese, softened
1 (14-ounce) can Eagle® Brand Sweetened Condensed Milk (NOT evaporated milk)
⅓ cup ReaLemon® Lemon Juice from Concentrate

In small mixer bowl, beat cheese until fluffy. Gradually beat in sweetened condensed milk until smooth. Stir in ReaLemon. Chill 1 hour. Use to frost one (13x9-inch) cake *or* one (15x10-inch) sheet cake *or* 2½ dozen cupcakes. Store in refrigerator.

CRUNCHY LEMON SQUARES

Makes 9 servings

1 cup unsifted flour
1 cup quick-cooking oats
½ cup coarsely chopped pecans
½ cup firmly packed light brown sugar
½ cup flaked coconut
1 teaspoon baking powder
½ cup margarine or butter, melted
1 (14-ounce) can Eagle® Brand Sweetened Condensed Milk (NOT evaporated milk)
½ cup ReaLemon® Lemon Juice from Concentrate
1 tablespoon grated lemon rind

Preheat oven to 350° (325° for glass dish). In medium mixing bowl, combine flour, oats, nuts, sugar, coconut, baking powder and margarine; stir until crumbly. Set aside. In medium mixing bowl, combine sweetened condensed milk, ReaLemon and rind. Press half the crumb mixture evenly on bottom of 9-inch square baking pan. Spread sweetened condensed milk mixture on top; sprinkle with remaining crumbs. Bake 25 to 30 minutes or until lightly browned. Cool. Chill thoroughly. Cut into squares; garnish as desired. Refrigerate leftovers.

EASY LEMON PUDDING

Makes 6 to 8 servings

1 (14-ounce) can Eagle® Brand Sweetened Condensed Milk (NOT evaporated milk)
2½ cups cold water
2 (3¾-ounce) packages instant lemon pudding and pie filling mix

In large mixing bowl, combine sweetened condensed milk and water. Add pudding mix; beat until well blended. Chill thoroughly. Serve in individual dessert dishes or fill 12 medium-size cream puffs. Refrigerate leftovers.

BUTTERSCOTCH APPLE SQUARES

Makes 12 servings

¼ cup margarine or butter
1½ cups graham cracker crumbs
2 small all-purpose apples, pared and chopped (about 1¼ cups)
1 (6-ounce) package butter-scotch flavored chips
1 (14-ounce) can Eagle® Brand Sweetened Condensed Milk (NOT evaporated milk)
1 (3½-ounce) can flaked coconut (1⅓ cups)
1 cup chopped nuts

Continued next column

Butterscotch Apple Squares

Preheat oven to 350° (325° for glass dish). In 3-quart shallow baking pan (13x9-inch), melt margarine in oven. Sprinkle crumbs evenly over margarine; top with apples. In heavy saucepan, over medium heat, melt chips with sweetened condensed milk. Pour butterscotch mixture evenly over apples. Top with coconut and nuts; press down firmly. Bake 25 to 30 minutes or until lightly browned. Cool. Chill thoroughly. Garnish as desired. Refrigerate leftovers.

MICROWAVE: In 2½-quart shallow baking dish (12x7-inch), microwave margarine on full power (high) 1 minute or until melted. Sprinkle crumbs evenly over margarine; top with apples. In 1-quart glass measure, microwave chips with sweetened condensed milk on ⅔ power (medium-high) 2 to 3 minutes. Mix well. Pour butterscotch mixture evenly over apples. Top with coconut and nuts. Press down firmly. Microwave on full power (high) 8 to 9 minutes. Proceed as above.

FUDGY MILK CHOCOLATE FONDUE ▲

Makes about 3 cups

1 (16-ounce) can chocolate
    flavored syrup
1 (14-ounce) can Eagle® Brand
    Sweetened Condensed Milk
    (NOT evaporated milk)
    Dash salt
1½ teaspoons vanilla extract
    Dippers*

In heavy saucepan, combine syrup,
sweetened condensed milk and salt.
Over medium heat, cook and stir 12 to
15 minutes or until slightly thickened.
Remove from heat; stir in vanilla. Serve
warm with Dippers. Refrigerate
leftovers.

Tip: Can be served warm or cold over
ice cream. Can be made several weeks
ahead. Store tightly covered in
refrigerator.

Continued next column

Fudgy Milk Chocolate Fondue

MICROWAVE: In 1-quart glass measure,
combine syrup, sweetened condensed
milk and salt. Microwave on full power
(high) 3½ to 4 minutes, stirring after
2 minutes. Stir in vanilla.

*Dippers: pound cake cubes, melon
balls, cherries with stems, pineapple
chunks, orange slices, strawberries,
banana slices, apple wedges, grapes,
dried apricots, peach chunks, plum
slices, pear slices, angel food cake
cubes, kiwifruit slices and marshmallows.

GOLDEN BREAD PUDDING

Makes 6 to 8 servings

**3 cups soft white bread cubes
(4 slices bread)**
3 eggs
3 cups warm water
**1 (14-ounce) can Eagle® Brand
Sweetened Condensed Milk
(NOT evaporated milk)**
**2 tablespoons margarine or
butter, melted**
½ teaspoon salt
1 teaspoon vanilla extract

Preheat oven to 350°. Place bread
cubes in buttered 9-inch square baking
pan. In large mixing bowl, beat eggs;
stir in remaining ingredients. Pour
evenly over bread cubes, completely
moistening bread. Bake 45 to 50
minutes or until knife inserted in center
comes out clean. Cool. Serve warm or
chilled. Refrigerate leftovers.

Tip: For firmer bread pudding, increase
bread cubes to 4 cups.

Apple Bread Pudding: Decrease water
to 1¾ cups; increase margarine to
¼ cup and add 1 teaspoon ground
cinnamon. In buttered 9-inch square
baking pan, combine 4 cups bread
cubes (5 slices bread), 2 cups pared,
chopped all-purpose apples (3 medium)
and ½ cup raisins. Proceed as above.

Pineapple Bread Pudding: Reduce
water to 2¾ cups. Add 1 (8-ounce) can
crushed pineapple, undrained. Proceed
as above.

Blueberry 'n' Spice Bread Pudding:
Reduce water to 1½ cups; increase
margarine to ¼ cup. Add 2 cups fresh
or dry-pack frozen blueberries to bread
cubes. Add ½ teaspoon ground cinnamon and ½ teaspoon ground nutmeg.
Proceed as above.

CREAMY DUTCH APPLE DESSERT

Makes 10 to 12 servings

¼ cup margarine or butter
1½ cups graham cracker crumbs
**1 (14-ounce) can Eagle® Brand
Sweetened Condensed Milk
(NOT evaporated milk)**
1 (8-ounce) container sour cream
**¼ cup ReaLemon® Lemon Juice
from Concentrate**
1 (21-ounce) can apple pie filling
¼ cup chopped walnuts
¼ teaspoon ground cinnamon

Preheat oven to 350°. In 1½-quart
shallow baking dish (10x6-inch), melt
margarine in oven. Sprinkle crumbs
over margarine; mix well. Press firmly
on bottom of dish. In medium mixing
bowl, combine sweetened condensed
milk, sour cream and ReaLemon;
spread evenly over crumbs. Spoon pie
filling evenly over creamy layer. Bake
25 to 30 minutes or until set. Cool
slightly. Before serving, in small dish,
stir together nuts and cinnamon;
sprinkle over apple layer. Serve warm
or chilled. Refrigerate leftovers.

CREAMY BANANA PUDDING

Makes 8 to 10 servings

1 (14-ounce) can Eagle® Brand Sweetened Condensed Milk (NOT evaporated milk)
1½ cups cold water
1 (3½-ounce) package instant vanilla pudding and pie filling mix
2 cups (1 pint) whipping cream, whipped
36 vanilla wafers
3 medium bananas, sliced and dipped in lemon juice

In large mixing bowl, combine sweetened condensed milk and water. Add pudding mix; beat until well blended. Chill 5 minutes. Fold in whipped cream. Spoon *1 cup* pudding mixture into 2½-quart round glass serving bowl. Top with one-third each of the vanilla wafers, bananas and pudding. Repeat layering twice, ending with pudding mixture. Chill thoroughly. Garnish as desired. Refrigerate leftovers.

Tip: Mixture can be layered in individual serving dishes.

CHERRY ALMOND CREAM DESSERT

Makes 10 to 12 servings

1 (14-ounce) can Eagle® Brand Sweetened Condensed Milk (NOT evaporated milk)
1½ cups cold water
1 (3½-ounce) package instant vanilla pudding and pie filling mix
1 teaspoon almond extract
2 cups (1 pint) whipping cream, whipped
1 (10¾- *or* 12-ounce) prepared loaf pound cake, cut into 10 slices
1 (21-ounce) can cherry pie filling, chilled
Toasted almonds

In large mixing bowl, combine sweetened condensed milk and water. Add pudding mix and extract; beat until well blended. Chill 5 minutes. Fold in whipped cream. Spoon half the cream mixture into 13x9-inch baking dish; top with cake slices, pie filling, remaining cream mixture then almonds. Chill thoroughly. Refrigerate leftovers.

Creamy Banana Pudding

ORANGE NUT CREAM DESSERTS ▲

Makes 6 to 8 servings

1 (14-ounce) can Eagle® Brand
   Sweetened Condensed Milk
   (NOT evaporated milk)
1 (6-ounce) can frozen orange
   juice concentrate, thawed
1 (8-ounce) container sour cream
1 cup flaked coconut
½ cup chopped pecans
1 tablespoon grated orange rind
   Orange sections

In medium mixing bowl, combine
sweetened condensed milk and juice
concentrate. Stir in sour cream. In
small bowl, combine coconut, nuts and
rind. Layer filling, coconut mixture then
orange sections in dessert dishes.
Repeat, ending with coconut mixture
and orange sections. Chill at least
2 hours. Refrigerate leftovers.

MAGIC-QUICK CHOCOLATE FROSTING

Makes about 1½ cups

2 (1-ounce) squares unsweetened
   chocolate
1 (14-ounce) can Eagle® Brand
   Sweetened Condensed Milk
   (NOT evaporated milk)
   Dash salt
1 tablespoon water
½ teaspoon vanilla extract

In heavy saucepan, over medium heat,
melt chocolate with sweetened condensed milk and salt. Cook and stir until
mixture thickens, about 10 minutes.
Remove from heat. Stir in water; cool.
Stir in vanilla. Use to frost one (8- or
9-inch) two-layer cake or one (13x9-
inch) cake. Store at room temperature.

MICROWAVE: In 1-quart glass measure,
combine chocolate, sweetened condensed
milk and salt. Microwave on full power
(high) 3 minutes, stirring after 1½ minutes. Stir until smooth. Proceed as above.

BAKED ALMOND PUDDING

Makes 8 to 10 servings

¼ cup firmly packed brown sugar
¾ cup slivered almonds, toasted
1 (14-ounce) can Eagle® Brand
   Sweetened Condensed Milk
   (NOT evaporated milk)
5 eggs
1 cup (½ pint) whipping cream
½ teaspoon almond extract
   Additional toasted almonds,
   optional

Preheat oven to 325°. In 8-inch round layer cake pan, sprinkle sugar; set aside. In blender or food processor container, grind nuts; add sweetened condensed milk, eggs, ½ cup cream and extract. Blend thoroughly. Pour into prepared pan; set in larger pan. Fill pan with 1 inch hot water. Bake 40 to 45 minutes or until knife inserted near center comes out clean. Cool. Chill thoroughly; invert onto serving plate. Beat remaining cream for garnish; top with additional almonds if desired. Refrigerate leftovers.

CARAMEL FLAN

Makes 10 to 12 servings

¾ cup sugar
4 eggs
1¾ cups water
1 (14-ounce) can Eagle® Brand
   Sweetened Condensed Milk
   (NOT evaporated milk)
½ teaspoon vanilla extract
⅛ teaspoon salt

Preheat oven to 350°. In heavy skillet, over medium heat, cook sugar, stirring constantly until melted and caramel-colored. Pour into 9-inch round layer cake pan, tilting to coat bottom completely. In medium mixing bowl, beat eggs; stir in water, sweetened condensed milk, vanilla and salt. Pour into carmelized pan; set in larger pan (a broiler pan). Fill pan with 1 inch hot water. Bake 55 to 60 minutes or until knife inserted near center comes out clean. Cool. Chill thoroughly. Loosen side of flan with knife; invert onto serving plate with rim. Garnish as desired. Refrigerate leftovers.

FRUIT GLAZED BAKED CUSTARDS

Makes 6 servings

3 eggs
1 (14-ounce) can Eagle® Brand
   Sweetened Condensed Milk
   (NOT evaporated milk)
1 cup water
1 teaspoon vanilla extract
½ cup red currant jelly
2 tablespoons orange-flavored
   liqueur or orange juice
1 tablespoon cornstarch
   Few drops red food coloring,
   optional
   Fresh strawberries or other
   fruit

Preheat oven to 350°. In medium mixing bowl, beat eggs; stir in sweetened condensed milk, water and vanilla. Pour equal portions of mixture into six 6-ounce custard cups. Set cups in shallow pan; fill pan with 1 inch hot water. Bake 45 to 50 minutes or until knife inserted in center comes out clean. Cool. In small saucepan, combine jelly, liqueur and cornstarch. Cook and stir until jelly melts and mixture comes to a boil. Stir in food coloring if desired. Cool to room temperature. Invert custards onto serving plates. Top with sauce and strawberries. Refrigerate leftovers.

Pictured Top to Bottom: Baked Almond Pudding, Caramel Flan, Fruit Glazed Baked Custards.

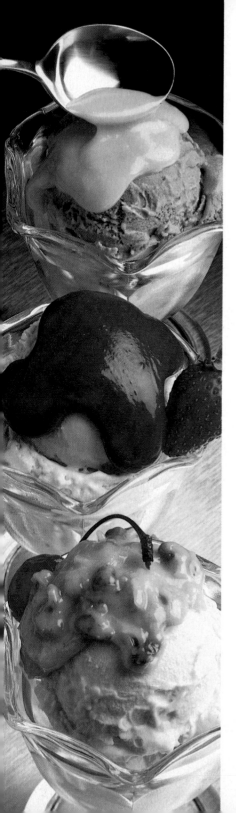

HOT FUDGE SAUCE

Makes about 1½ cups

1 (6-ounce) package semi-sweet chocolate chips *or* **4 (1-ounce) squares semi-sweet chocolate**
2 tablespoons margarine or butter
1 (14-ounce) can Eagle® Brand Sweetened Condensed Milk (NOT evaporated milk)
Dash salt
1 teaspoon vanilla extract

In heavy saucepan, over medium heat, melt chips and margarine with sweetened condensed milk and salt. Cook, stirring constantly, until sauce is slightly thickened, about 5 minutes. Remove from heat; stir in vanilla. Serve warm over ice cream. Refrigerate leftovers.

MICROWAVE: In 1-quart glass measure, combine chips and margarine. Microwave on full power (high) 1 minute; stir. Add remaining ingredients; mix well. Microwave on full power (high) 2 to 2½ minutes, stirring after each minute.

To Reheat: In small heavy saucepan, combine desired amout of sauce with small amount of water. Over low heat, stir constantly until heated through.

Variations

Mocha: Add 1 teaspoon instant coffee to chips and margarine. Proceed as above.

Toasted Almond: Omit vanilla extract. Add ½ teaspoon almond extract. When sauce is thickened, stir in ½ cup chopped toasted almonds.

Choco-Mint: Omit vanilla extract. Add ½ to 1 teaspoon peppermint extract. Proceed as above.

Spirited: Add ⅓ cup almond, coffee, mint *or* orange-flavored liqueur after mixture has thickened.

Mexican: Add 2 tablespoons coffee-flavored liqueur *or* 1 teaspoon instant coffee dissolved in 2 tablespoons water and 1 teaspoon ground cinnamon after mixture has thickened.

Pictured Top to Bottom: Peanut Butter Sauce, Hot Fudge Sauce, Coconut Pecan Sauce.

PEANUT BUTTER SAUCE

Makes about 1½ cups

**1 (14-ounce) can Eagle® Brand
 Sweetened Condensed Milk
 (NOT evaporated milk)
¼ to ⅓ cup peanut butter
 Chopped peanuts, optional**

In heavy saucepan, over low heat,
combine sweetened condensed milk
and peanut butter; cook and stir until
well blended. Stir in nuts if desired.
Serve warm over ice cream. Refrigerate
leftovers.

MICROWAVE: In 1-quart glass measure,
combine sweetened condensed milk
and peanut butter. Microwave on full
power (high) 2½ to 3½ minutes, stirring
after each minute. Proceed as above.

To Reheat: In small heavy saucepan,
combine desired amount of sauce with
small amount of water. Over low heat,
stir constantly until heated through.

COCONUT PECAN SAUCE

Makes about 2 cups

**1 (14-ounce) can Eagle® Brand
 Sweetened Condensed Milk
 (NOT evaporated milk)
2 egg yolks, beaten
¼ cup margarine or butter
½ cup flaked coconut
½ cup chopped pecans
1 teaspoon vanilla extract**

In heavy saucepan, combine sweetened
condensed milk, egg yolks and margarine. Over medium heat, cook and
stir until thickened and bubbly, about
8 minutes. Stir in remaining ingredients.
Serve warm over ice cream or cake.

MICROWAVE: In 1-quart glass measure,
combine sweetened condensed milk,
egg yolks and margarine. Microwave on
⅔ power (medium-high) 3 minutes; stir.
Microwave on ⅔ power (medium-high)
1 to 2 minutes. Proceed as above.

To Reheat: In small heavy saucepan,
combine desired amount of sauce with
small amount of water. Over low heat,
stir constantly until heated through.

CREAMY PECAN RUM SAUCE

Makes about 1½ cups

**¼ cup margarine or butter
1 (14-ounce) can Eagle® Brand
 Sweetened Condensed Milk
 (NOT evaporated milk)
½ teaspoon rum flavoring
 Dash salt
¼ cup chopped pecans**

In small saucepan, over medium heat,
melt margarine; add remaining ingredients. Cook and stir until slightly
thickened, 10 to 12 minutes. Cool
10 minutes. *Sauce thickens as it cools.*
Serve warm over baked apples, fruit or
ice cream. Refrigerate leftovers.

MICROWAVE: In 1-quart glass measure,
microwave margarine on full power
(high) 1 minute or until melted. Stir in
remaining ingredients. Microwave on
⅔ power (medium-high) 3 to 3½
minutes. Proceed as above.

To Reheat: In small heavy saucepan,
combine desired amount of sauce with
small amount of water. Over low heat,
stir constantly until heated through.

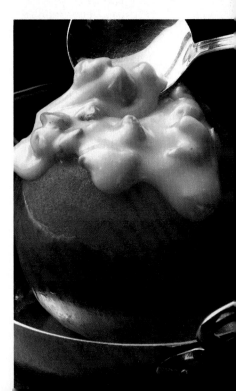

Creamy Pecan Rum Sauce

Makes 8 to 10 servings

2 cups quick-cooking oats
1½ cups unsifted flour
½ teaspoon baking soda
½ teaspoon salt
1 cup margarine or butter, softened
1 cup firmly packed light brown sugar
1 teaspoon vanilla extract
1 pound yams or sweet potatoes, cooked, peeled and mashed *or* 1 (16- or 17-ounce) can yams, drained and mashed (about *2* cups)
1 (14-ounce) can Eagle® Brand Sweetened Condensed Milk (NOT evaporated milk)
2 eggs, beaten
1½ teaspoons ground allspice *or* pumpkin pie spice
1 teaspoon grated orange rind
½ cup chopped nuts

Preheat oven to 350°. Combine oats, flour, baking soda and salt; set aside. In large mixer bowl, beat margarine, sugar and vanilla until fluffy. Add dry ingredients; mix until crumbly. Reserving *1 cup* crumb mixture, press remainder firmly on bottom of 13x9-inch baking dish. Bake 10 minutes. Meanwhile, in large mixing bowl, combine remaining ingredients except nuts; mix well. Pour over prepared crust. Combine nuts with reserved crumb mixture; crumble evenly over top. Bake 25 to 30 minutes or until golden brown. Cool. Serve warm or chilled. Garnish as desired. Refrigerate leftovers.

Tip: 1 (16-ounce) can pumpkin can be substituted for yams.

PUMPKIN RUM CUSTARDS

Makes 8 to 10 servings

1 cup sugar
4 eggs
1 (14-ounce) can Eagle® Brand Sweetened Condensed Milk (NOT evaporated milk)
1½ cups water
1 (16-ounce) can pumpkin (about 2 cups)
⅓ cup light rum
½ teaspoon ground nutmeg
½ teaspoon salt
⅛ to ¼ teaspoon ground ginger

Preheat oven to 350°. In heavy skillet, over medium heat, cook sugar, stirring constantly until melted and caramel-colored. Using eight to ten 6-ounce custard cups, pour about 1 tablespoon carmelized sugar on bottom of each. In large mixer bowl, beat eggs; stir in remaining ingredients. Pour equal portions of mixture into prepared cups. Set cups in shallow pan; fill pan with 1 inch hot water. Bake 50 to 60 minutes or until knife inserted in center comes out clean. Cool. Chill thoroughly. Invert custards onto serving plates. Garnish as desired. Refrigerate leftovers.

STRAWBERRY CHIFFON SQUARES

Makes 12 servings

1 ½ cups vanilla wafer crumbs
    (about 45 wafers)
⅓ cup margarine or butter, melted
1 (3-ounce) package strawberry
    flavor gelatin
¾ cup boiling water
1 (14-ounce) can Eagle® Brand
    Sweetened Condensed Milk
    (NOT evaporated milk)
1 (10-ounce) package frozen
    sliced strawberries in syrup,
    thawed
4 cups Campfire® Miniature
    Marshmallows
1 cup (½ pint) whipping cream,
    whipped

Combine crumbs and margarine; press firmly on bottom of 12x7-inch baking dish. In large mixing bowl, dissolve gelatin in water; stir in sweetened condensed milk and undrained strawberries. Fold in marshmallows and whipped cream. Pour into prepared dish. Chill 2 hours or until set. Garnish as desired. Refrigerate leftovers.

LIME CHIFFON SQUARES

Makes 10 to 12 servings

¼ cup margarine or butter, melted
1 cup graham cracker crumbs
1 (3-ounce) package lime flavor
    gelatin
1 cup boiling water
1 (14-ounce) can Eagle® Brand
    Sweetened Condensed Milk
    (NOT evaporated milk)
1 (8-ounce) can crushed pine-
    apple, undrained
2 tablespoons ReaLime® Lime
    Juice from Concentrate
4 cups Campfire® Miniature
    Marshmallows
1 cup (½ pint) whipping cream,
    whipped

Combine margarine and crumbs; press firmly on bottom of 9-inch square *or* 12x7-inch baking dish. In large mixing bowl, dissolve gelatin in water; stir in sweetened condensed milk, pineapple and ReaLime. Fold in marshmallows and whipped cream. Pour into prepared dish. Chill 2 hours or until set. Garnish as desired. Refrigerate leftovers.

Lime Chiffon Square

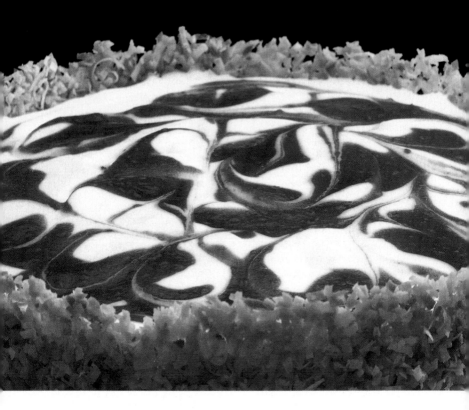

RASPBERRY SWIRL DESSERT

Makes 10 to 12 servings

1 (7-ounce) package flaked
   coconut, toasted (2⅔ cups)
⅓ cup margarine or butter, melted
1 (10-ounce) package frozen red
   raspberries in syrup, thawed
1 tablespoon cornstarch
1 envelope unflavored gelatine
¼ cup water
1 (14-ounce) can Eagle® Brand
   Sweetened Condensed Milk
   (NOT evaporated milk)
1 (8-ounce) container sour cream
3 tablespoons orange-flavored
   liqueur
1 cup (½ pint) whipping cream,
   stiffly whipped

Continued next column

Raspberry Swirl Dessert

Combine coconut and margarine; press firmly on bottom and up side of 8- or 9-inch springform pan. Chill. In blender container, blend raspberries until smooth. In small saucepan, combine raspberries and cornstarch; cook and stir until mixture thickens. Cool to room temperature. Meanwhile, in small saucepan, sprinkle gelatine over water; let stand 1 minute. Over low heat, stir until gelatine dissolves; set aside. In large mixing bowl, combine sweetened condensed milk, sour cream, liqueur and gelatine; mix well. Fold in whipped cream. Chill 10 minutes or until mixture mounds slightly. Spread half the gelatine mixture into prepared pan; top with half the raspberry mixture in small amounts. Repeat layering. With metal spatula, swirl raspberry mixture through cream mixture. Chill 6 hours or until set. Garnish as desired. Refrigerate leftovers.

Raspberry Swirl Charlotte: Omit coconut and margarine. Line bottom and side of springform pan with 28 ladyfinger halves. Proceed as above.

FLOATING ISLAND LIME DESSERTS

Makes 4 servings

Floating Islands*
1 (14-ounce) can Eagle® Brand
    Sweetened Condensed Milk
    (NOT evaporated milk)
2 egg yolks**
½ cup ReaLime® Lime Juice from
    Concentrate
2 to 3 drops green food coloring,
    optional
2 tablespoons flaked coconut,
    toasted

Prepare Floating Islands. Meanwhile, in
medium mixing bowl, beat sweetened
condensed milk and egg yolks; stir in
ReaLime and food coloring if desired.
Spoon into four 6-ounce dessert
dishes. Top each with a Floating Island.
Chill 2 hours or until set. Garnish with
coconut. Refrigerate leftovers.

*Floating Islands: In small mixer bowl,
beat 2 egg whites** until soft peaks
form. Gradually beat in 2 tablespoons
sugar, beating until stiff but not dry.
Drop one-fourth of mixture onto
simmering water in large skillet;
repeat to make 4 islands. Simmer
uncovered 5 minutes or until meringues
are set. Remove with slotted spoon;
drain on paper towels.

**Use only Grade A clean, uncracked
eggs.

CREAMY RICE PUDDING

Makes 8 to 10 servings

2 cups uncooked long grain rice,
    cooked
1 (14-ounce) can Eagle® Brand
    Sweetened Condensed Milk
    (NOT evaporated milk)
2 egg yolks
¼ cup water
½ teaspoon ground cinnamon
½ cup raisins
2 teaspoons vanilla extract

In large saucepan, combine sweetened
condensed milk, egg yolks, water and
cinnamon. Over medium heat, cook
and stir until mixture thickens slightly,
10 to 15 minutes. Remove from heat;
add cooked rice, raisins and vanilla.
Cool. Chill thoroughly. Refrigerate
leftovers.

Floating Island Lime Dessert

ICE CREAM & FROZEN DESSERTS

FROM THE DESSERT MAKER

Pictured: Easy
Homemade French Vanilla
Ice Cream, Easy Homemade
Chocolate Ice Cream, Peppermint
Ice Cream Loaf (recipes page 88).

PEPPERMINT ICE CREAM LOAF

Makes 8 to 10 servings

2 cups finely crushed creme-filled chocolate sandwich cookies (about 20 cookies)
3 tablespoons margarine or butter, melted
1 cup crushed hard peppermint candy
¼ cup water
1 (14-ounce) can Eagle® Brand Sweetened Condensed Milk (NOT evaporated milk)
3 egg yolks*
1 to 2 drops red food coloring, optional
2 cups (1 pint) whipping cream, whipped *(do not use non-dairy whipped topping)*

Line 9x5-inch loaf pan with aluminum foil, extending foil above sides of pan. Combine crumbs and margarine; press firmly on bottom and halfway up sides of prepared pan. In blender container, blend ¼ *cup* peppermint candy and water until candy dissolves. In large mixer bowl, beat sweetened condensed milk, egg yolks, food coloring if desired, ½ *cup* crushed candy and peppermint liquid until well blended. Fold in whipped cream and remaining ¼ *cup* crushed candy. Pour into prepared pan. Cover; freeze 6 hours or overnight. Garnish as desired. To serve, remove from pan; peel off foil and slice. Return leftovers to freezer.

*Use only Grade A clean, uncracked eggs.

EASY HOMEMADE FRENCH VANILLA ICE CREAM

Makes about 1½ quarts

1 (14-ounce) can Eagle® Brand Sweetened Condensed Milk (NOT evaporated milk)
3 egg yolks*, beaten
4 teaspoons vanilla extract
2 cups (1 pint) whipping cream, whipped *(do not use non-dairy whipped topping)*

Continued next column

Easy Homemade French Vanilla Ice Cream

In large mixer bowl, beat sweetened condensed milk, egg yolks and vanilla until well blended. Fold in whipped cream. Pour into 9x5-inch loaf pan or other 2-quart container; cover. Freeze 6 hours or until firm. Return leftovers to freezer.

Vanilla Nut: Add ¾ cup chopped nuts. Proceed as above.

Coffee: Dissolve 1 tablespoon instant coffee in 1 teaspoon hot water; add to ice cream mixture. Proceed as above.

Chocolate Chip: Add ½ cup mini chocolate chips. Proceed as above.

Ice Cream 'n' Cookies: Fold in 1 cup coarsely crushed chocolate sandwich cookies. Proceed as above.

*Use only Grade A clean, uncracked eggs.

EASY HOMEMADE CHOCOLATE ICE CREAM

Makes about 1½ quarts

1 (14-ounce) can Eagle® Brand Sweetened Condensed Milk (NOT evaporated milk)
⅔ cup chocolate flavored syrup
2 cups (1 pint) whipping cream, whipped *(do not use non-dairy whipped topping)*

In large mixing bowl, combine sweetened condensed milk and syrup. Fold in whipped cream. Pour into 9x5-inch loaf pan or other 2-quart container; cover. Freeze 6 hours or until firm. Return leftovers to freezer.

Chocolate Mocha: Add 1 tablespoon instant coffee to sweetened condensed milk and syrup. Let stand 10 minutes. Proceed as above.

Chocolate Peanut Butter: Add ½ cup peanut butter. Proceed as above.

Chocolate Nut: Add ¾ cup chopped nuts. Proceed as above.

Chocolate Rocky Road: Add ½ cup chopped peanuts and 1 cup Campfire® Miniature Marshmallows. Proceed as above.

Chocolate Mint: Add 1 teaspoon peppermint extract. Proceed as above.

Chocolate Chocolate Chip: Add ¾ cup mini chocolate chips. Proceed as above.

MUD PIE

Makes one 9-inch pie ▲

1 (14-ounce) can Eagle® Brand
Sweetened Condensed Milk
(NOT evaporated milk)
3 egg yolks*
4 teaspoons vanilla extract
1 cup coarsely crushed creme-
filled chocolate sandwich
cookies (12 cookies)
2 cups (1 pint) whipping cream,
whipped (do not use non-
dairy whipped topping)
1 (9-inch) chocolate crumb crust
Chocolate fudge ice cream
topping or chocolate
flavored syrup
Chopped nuts

In large mixer bowl, beat sweetened
condensed milk, egg yolks and vanilla
until well blended. Fold in cookies and
whipped cream. Pour into 9x5-inch loaf
pan or other 2-quart container; cover.
Freeze 6 hours or until firm. Scoop ice
cream into prepared crust. Drizzle with
topping. Garnish with nuts. Return
leftovers to freezer.

*Use only Grade A clean, uncracked
eggs.

LEMON DESSERT FREEZE

Makes 9 servings

3 tablespoons margarine or
butter, melted
1 cup graham cracker crumbs
1 (21- or 22-ounce) can lemon
pie filling
1 (14-ounce) can Eagle® Brand
Sweetened Condensed Milk
(NOT evaporated milk)
½ cup ReaLemon® Lemon Juice
from Concentrate
1½ cups frozen non-dairy whipped
topping, thawed

Combine margarine and crumbs.
Reserving 1 tablespoon crumbs for
garnish, press remainder firmly on
bottom of 8- or 9-inch square pan; set
aside. In medium mixing bowl, combine
pie filling, sweetened condensed milk
and ReaLemon; stir until smooth.
Spread into prepared pan. Spread
whipped topping over top; garnish with
reserved crumbs. Freeze 4 hours or
until firm. Garnish as desired. Cut into
squares to serve. Return leftovers to
freezer.

FROZEN FLUFFY STRAWBERRY PIE

Makes one 9-inch pie

2½ cups flaked coconut, toasted
⅓ cup margarine or butter, melted
1 (3-ounce) package cream cheese, softened
1 (14-ounce) can Eagle® Brand Sweetened Condensed Milk (NOT evaporated milk)
2½ cups fresh or frozen unsweetened strawberries, thawed, mashed or pureed (about 1½ cups)
3 tablespoons ReaLemon® Lemon Juice from Concentrate
1 cup (½ pint) whipping cream, whipped
Additional fresh strawberries, optional

Continued next column

Frozen Fluffy Strawberry Pie

Combine coconut and margarine; press firmly on bottom and up side to rim of 9-inch pie plate. In large mixer bowl, beat cheese until fluffy; gradually beat in sweetened condensed milk. Stir in pureed strawberries and ReaLemon. Fold in whipped cream. Pour into prepared crust (mixture should mound slightly). Freeze 4 hours or until firm. Before serving, garnish with fresh strawberries if desired. Return leftovers to freezer.

Tip: 1 (9-inch) baked pastry shell can be substituted for coconut crust.

EASY CHOCOLATE ICE CREAM 'N' CAKE

Makes 12 servings

1 (18½-ounce) package white cake mix
1 (14-ounce) can Eagle® Brand Sweetened Condensed Milk (NOT evaporated milk)
⅔ cup chocolate flavored syrup
1 cup slivered almonds, toasted and chopped, optional
2 cups (1 pint) whipping cream, whipped *(do not use non-dairy whipped topping)*
1 (8-ounce) container frozen non-dairy whipped topping, thawed
Additional chocolate flavored syrup

Prepare and bake cake mix as directed for 13x9-inch cake. Cool slightly. Turn out on sheet of aluminum foil. Cool thoroughly; set aside. In large mixing bowl, combine sweetened condensed milk, *⅔ cup* syrup and *1 cup* chopped almonds. Fold in whipped cream. Line 13x9-inch baking pan with aluminum foil, extending foil above sides of pan. Pour chocolate mixture into prepared pan; cover. Freeze 6 hours or until firm. Lift ice cream out of pan with foil; turn out evenly on top of cake layer. Trim ice cream to fit cake layer. Quickly frost top and sides with whipped topping. Drizzle with chocolate syrup. Return to freezer at least 2 hours before serving. Return leftovers to freezer.

Tip: Can be made 2 weeks ahead.

Peach Ice Cream

VANILLA ICE CREAM

Makes about 3 quarts

4 eggs*, well beaten
6 cups (1½ quarts) coffee cream
2 (14-ounce) cans Eagle® Brand
Sweetened Condensed Milk
(NOT evaporated milk)
2 tablespoons vanilla extract

In ice cream freezer container, combine ingredients; mix well. Freeze according to manufacturer's instructions. Return leftovers to freezer.

Peach Ice Cream: Reduce vanilla to 1 tablespoon and add 1 teaspoon almond extract, 4 drops yellow and 2 drops red food coloring if desired and 2 cups mashed fresh or frozen peaches, thawed or 1 (16-ounce) can peaches, drained and mashed. Proceed as above.

Strawberry Ice Cream: Omit eggs. Reduce vanilla to 1 tablespoon. Add 2 cups mashed fresh or frozen strawberries, thawed and few drops red food coloring if desired. Proceed as above.

Banana Ice Cream: Reduce vanilla to 1 tablespoon; add 2 cups mashed bananas (4 medium). Proceed as above.

*Use only Grade A clean, uncracked eggs.

FUDGY CHOCOLATE ICE CREAM

Makes about 1½ quarts

2 (1-ounce) squares unsweetened
***or* semi-sweet chocolate**
1 (14-ounce) can Eagle® Brand
Sweetened Condensed Milk
(NOT evaporated milk)
3 cups (1½ pints) coffee cream
1 tablespoon vanilla extract

In medium saucepan, over low heat, melt chocolate with sweetened condensed milk; continue cooking until mixture thickens. Remove from heat; cool. Add remaining ingredients; *mix well.* Place in ice cream freezer container. Freeze according to manufacturer's instructions. Return leftovers to freezer.

Refrigerator-Freezer Method: Place combined ingredients in 13x9-inch baking pan; cover and freeze to a firm mush, about 1 hour. Break into pieces and turn into chilled large mixer bowl; beat until smooth. Return to pan. Cover; freeze until firm.

Tip: Recipe can be doubled.

FROZEN MOCHA CHEESECAKE

Makes one 8- or 9-inch cheesecake

1¼ cups chocolate wafer cookie crumbs (about 24 wafers)
¼ cup margarine or butter, melted
¼ cup sugar
1 (8-ounce) package cream cheese, softened
1 (14-ounce) can Eagle® Brand Sweetened Condensed Milk (NOT evaporated milk)
⅔ cup chocolate flavored syrup
1 to 2 tablespoons instant coffee
1 teaspoon hot water
1 cup (½ pint) whipping cream, whipped
    Additional chocolate crumbs, optional

Continued next column

Frozen Mocha Cheesecake

Combine crumbs, margarine and sugar; press firmly on bottom and up side of 8- or 9-inch springform pan or 13x9-inch baking pan. In large mixer bowl, beat cheese until fluffy. Gradually beat in sweetened condensed milk and chocolate syrup until smooth. In small bowl, dissolve coffee in water; add to cheese mixture. Mix well. Fold in whipped cream. Pour into prepared pan; cover. Freeze 6 hours or overnight. Garnish with chocolate crumbs if desired. Return leftovers to freezer.

◄ TORTONI

Makes 1½ to 2 dozen

**1 (14-ounce) can Eagle® Brand
   Sweetened Condensed Milk
   (NOT evaporated milk)**
3 egg yolks*, beaten
¼ cup light rum
2 teaspoons vanilla extract
**⅔ cup coconut macaroon crumbs
   (about 5 macaroons)**
**½ to ¾ cup slivered almonds,
   toasted**
**⅓ to ½ cup chopped maraschino
   cherries**
**2 cups (1 pint) whipping cream,
   whipped**

In large mixing bowl, combine all
ingredients except whipped cream; mix
well. Fold in whipped cream. Fill 2½-
inch foil cups; cover. Freeze 6 hours or
until firm. Garnish as desired. Return
leftovers to freezer.

*Use only Grade A clean, uncracked
  eggs.

FROZEN ORANGE CREAM

Makes about 1 quart

2 cups (1 pint) coffee cream
**1 (14-ounce) can Eagle® Brand
   Sweetened Condensed Milk
   (NOT evaporated milk)**
**1 (6-ounce) can frozen orange
   juice concentrate, thawed**
1 cup cold water
1 teaspoon grated orange rind

In large mixing bowl, combine ingredients; mix well. Pour into 8-inch square
pan; cover. Freeze 4 hours or until firm.
Remove from freezer 5 minutes before
serving. Return leftovers to freezer.

Frozen Lemon Cream: Omit orange
juice concentrate and orange rind. Use
½ cup ReaLemon® Lemon Juice from
Concentrate and 1 teaspoon grated
lemon rind. Proceed as above.

SPIRITED MOCHA MOUSSE

Makes 10 to 12 servings

1 tablespoon instant coffee
1 teaspoon hot water
1 (6-ounce) package semi-sweet
   chocolate chips
1 (14-ounce) can Eagle® Brand
   Sweetened Condensed Milk
   (NOT evaporated milk)
¼ cup coffee-flavored liqueur,
   optional
2 cups (1 pint) whipping cream,
   whipped *(do not use non-
   dairy whipped topping)*

In small bowl, dissolve coffee in water;
set aside. In medium saucepan, melt
chips; remove from heat. Stir in sweetened condensed milk, coffee liquid
and liqueur; mix well. Fold in whipped
cream. Spoon about *½ cup* mixture into
6-ounce dessert dishes; cover. Freeze
2 hours or until firm. Garnish as desired.
Return leftovers to freezer.

Use spoon to spread chocolate
mixture to form cup.

Chocolate Cup with Orange Frozen
Passion.

FROZEN PASSION

Makes about 2 quarts

2 (14-ounce) cans Eagle® Brand
   Sweetened Condensed Milk
   (NOT evaporated milk)
2 (28-ounce) bottles *or* 4 (12-
   ounce) cans any flavor
   carbonated beverage

**Electric or Hand-Turned Ice Cream
Freezer Method:** In ice cream freezer
container, combine ingredients; mix
well. Freeze according to manufacturer's instructions. Return leftovers
to freezer.

Refrigerator-Freezer Method: In large
mixing bowl, combine ingredients;
blend well. Turn into 13x9-inch baking
pan; freeze to a firm mush, about 1 hour.
Break into pieces and turn into chilled
large mixer bowl. Beat until smooth.
Return to pan; cover with aluminum
foil. Freeze until firm.

CHOCOLATE ICE CREAM CUPS ▲

Makes about 1½ dozen

1 (12-ounce) package semi-
   sweet chocolate chips
1 (14-ounce) can Eagle® Brand
   Sweetened Condensed Milk
   (NOT evaporated milk)
1 cup finely ground pecans
   Ice cream, any flavor

In small saucepan, over low heat, melt
chips with sweetened condensed milk;
remove from heat. Stir in pecans. In
individual paper-lined muffin cups,
spread about 2 tablespoons chocolate
mixture. With spoon, spread chocolate
on bottom and up side of each cup.
Freeze 2 hours or until firm. Before
serving, remove paper liners. Fill with
ice cream. Store unfilled cups tightly
covered in freezer.

Pour ice cream mixture into aluminum foil-lined round bowl.

Invert ice cream layer on brownie layer; peel off foil.

Spread meringue completely over ice cream and brownie, sealing carefully to edge of brownie.

◄GRASSHOPPER BAKED ALASKA

Makes 12 to 15 servings

Ice Cream:

1 (14-ounce) can Eagle® Brand
   Sweetened Condensed Milk
   (NOT evaporated milk)
⅓ cup green creme de menthe
¼ cup white creme de cacao
2 cups (1 pint) whipping cream,
   whipped *(do not use non-
   dairy whipped topping)*
½ cup mini chocolate chips

Brownie:

1 (15- or 15½-ounce) package
   brownie mix

Meringue:

4 egg whites*
¼ teaspoon cream of tartar
½ cup sugar
1 tablespoon unsweetened
   cocoa

1. To prepare ice cream, in large mixing
bowl, combine sweetened condensed milk
and liqueurs. Fold in whipped cream and
chips. Pour into aluminum foil-lined 2- or
3-quart round mixing bowl. Cover; freeze
8 to 12 hours or until firm.

2. Prepare brownie mix according to
package directions. Pour into greased
8-inch round layer cake pan; bake
according to package directions.
Remove from pan; cool thoroughly.

3. Preheat oven to 500°. In large mixer
bowl, beat egg whites and cream of
tartar until soft peaks form. Gradually
beat in sugar combined with cocoa
until stiff but not dry. Place prepared
brownie layer on ovenproof plate,
wooden board or baking sheet. Remove
ice cream from bowl; invert onto
brownie layer. Trim to fit if desired.
Quickly spread meringue over ice cream
and brownie, sealing carefully to bottom
edge of brownie. Bake 2 to 3 minutes or
until lightly browned. Return to freezer;
freeze at least 6 hours before serving.
Return leftovers to freezer.

Tip: Alaska should be made several
days ahead.

*Use only Grade A clean, uncracked
 eggs.

LEMON ICEBOX CAKE

Makes 6 to 8 servings

1½ cups chocolate wafer cookie
   crumbs (about 30 wafers)
3 tablespoons margarine or
   butter, melted
¼ cup plus 3 tablespoons sugar
1 (14-ounce) can Eagle® Brand
   Sweetened Condensed Milk
   (NOT evaporated milk)
2 eggs*, separated
½ cup ReaLemon® Lemon Juice
   from Concentrate
1 tablespoon grated lemon rind,
   optional
1 cup (½ pint) whipping cream,
   whipped

Line 9x5-inch loaf pan with aluminum
foil, extending foil above sides of pan;
butter foil. Combine crumbs, margarine
and *3 tablespoons* sugar. Press firmly
on bottom and up sides of prepared
pan. In large mixer bowl, beat sweetened
condensed milk and egg yolks until
well blended. Add ReaLemon and rind
if desired. In small mixer bowl, beat egg
whites until soft peaks form; gradually
add remaining ¼ *cup* sugar; beating
until stiff but not dry. Fold into sweetened condensed milk mixture along
with whipped cream. Pour into prepared
pan; cover. Freeze at least 8 hours or
until firm. To serve, remove from pan;
peel off foil and slice. Return leftovers
to freezer.

*Use only Grade A clean, uncracked
 eggs.

FROZEN PEANUT BUTTER PIE ▲

Makes one 9- or 10-inch pie

1 Chocolate Crunch Crust*
1 (8-ounce) package cream
    cheese, softened
1 (14-ounce) can Eagle® Brand
    Sweetened Condensed Milk
    (NOT evaporated milk)
¾ cup peanut butter
2 tablespoons ReaLemon®
    Lemon Juice from
    Concentrate
1 teaspoon vanilla extract
1 cup (½ pint) whipping cream,
    whipped or 1 (4-ounce)
    container frozen non-dairy
    whipped topping, thawed
Chocolate fudge ice cream
    topping

In large mixer bowl, beat cheese until
fluffy; gradually beat in sweetened
condensed milk then peanut butter
until smooth. Stir in ReaLemon and
vanilla. Fold in whipped cream. Turn
into prepared crust. Drizzle topping
over pie. Freeze 4 hours or until firm.
Return leftovers to freezer.

*Chocolate Crunch Crust: In heavy
saucepan, over low heat, melt ⅓ cup
margarine or butter and 1 (6-ounce)
package semi-sweet chocolate chips.
Remove from heat; gently stir in 2½
cups oven-toasted rice cereal until
completely coated. Press on bottom and
up side of buttered 9-inch or 10-inch pie
plate. Chill 30 minutes.

FROZEN AMARETTO TORTE

Makes 12 to 15 servings

⅓ cup margarine or butter, melted
2 cups chocolate wafer cookie
    crumbs (about 40 wafers)
½ cup slivered almonds, toasted
    and chopped
1 (6-ounce) package butterscotch
    flavored chips
1 (14-ounce) can Eagle® Brand
    Sweetened Condensed Milk
    (NOT evaporated milk)
1 (16-ounce) container sour
    cream
⅓ cup amaretto or other almond-
    flavored liqueur
1 cup (½ pint) whipping cream,
    whipped

Combine margarine, crumbs and
almonds. Reserving 1½ cups crumbs,
press remainder firmly on bottom of
9-inch springform pan. In small saucepan, over medium heat, melt chips with
sweetened condensed milk. In large
mixing bowl, combine sour cream and
amaretto; mix well. Stir in butterscotch
mixture. Fold in whipped cream. Pour
half the amaretto mixture over prepared
crust; top with 1 cup reserved crumbs
then remaining amaretto mixture. Top
with remaining ½ cup crumbs; cover.
Freeze 6 hours or until firm. Return
leftovers to freezer.

FROZEN STRAWBERRY MARGARITA PIE

Makes one 9-inch pie

1¼ cups *finely* crushed pretzel
    crumbs
½ cup plus 2 tablespoons
    margarine or butter, melted
¼ cup sugar
1 (14-ounce) can Eagle® Brand
    Sweetened Condensed Milk
    (NOT evaporated milk)
1 cup chopped fresh or frozen
    unsweetened strawberries,
    thawed
¼ cup ReaLime® Lime Juice from
    Concentrate
3 to 4 tablespoons tequila
2 tablespoons triple sec or other
    orange-flavored liqueur
2 to 4 drops red food coloring,
    optional
1 cup (½ pint) whipping cream,
    whipped

Continued next column

Frozen Strawberry Margarita Pie, Margarita Pie

Frozen Strawberry Margarita Pie

Combine crumbs, margarine and sugar; press firmly on bottom and up side of lightly buttered 9-inch pie plate. In large mixing bowl, combine sweetened condensed milk, chopped strawberries, ReaLime, tequila, triple sec and food coloring if desired; mix well. Fold in whipped cream. Pour into prepared crust. Freeze 4 hours or until firm. Let stand 10 minutes before serving. Garnish as desired. Return leftovers to freezer.

Margarita Pie: Omit strawberries and red food coloring. Increase ReaLime to ⅓ cup. Proceed as above. Freeze 4 hours or chill 2 hours. Garnish as desired. Return leftovers to freezer or refrigerator.

Pictured Clockwise From Top:
Coconut Rum Balls,
Chocolate Pecan Critters
(recipes page 104), Fruit Bon
Bons (recipe page 103), Milk
Chocolate Bourbon Balls, Buckeyes
(recipes page 104), Foolproof Creamy
Dark Chocolate Fudge (recipe page 102),
Peanut Butter Logs (recipe page 105),
Layered Mint Chocolate Candy (recipe page 103),
Creamy White Cherry Fudge (recipe page 102).

CANDIES & CONFECTIONS

FROM THE DESSERT MAKER

FOOLPROOF DARK CHOCOLATE FUDGE

Makes about 2 pounds

3 (6-ounce) packages semi-sweet chocolate chips
1 (14-ounce) can Eagle® Brand Sweetened Condensed Milk (NOT evaporated milk)
Dash salt
½ to 1 cup chopped nuts
1½ teaspoons vanilla extract

In heavy saucepan, over low heat, melt chips with sweetened condensed milk and salt. Remove from heat; stir in nuts and vanilla. Spread evenly into wax paper-lined 8- or 9-inch square pan. Chill 2 hours or until firm. Turn fudge onto cutting board; peel off paper and cut into squares. Store loosely covered at room temperature.

MICROWAVE: In 1-quart glass measure, combine chips with sweetened condensed milk. Microwave on full power (high) 3 minutes. Stir until chips melt and mixture is smooth. Stir in remaining ingredients. Proceed as above.

Creamy Dark Chocolate Fudge: Melt 2 cups Campfire® Miniature Marshmallows with chips and sweetened condensed milk. Proceed as above.

Milk Chocolate Fudge: Omit 1 (6-ounce) package semi-sweet chocolate chips. Add 1 cup milk chocolate chips. Proceed as above.

Creamy Milk Chocolate Fudge: Omit 1 (6-ounce) package semi-sweet chocolate chips. Add 1 cup milk chocolate chips and 2 cups Campfire® Miniature Marshmallows. Proceed as above.

Mexican Chocolate Fudge: Reduce vanilla to 1 teaspoon. Add 1 tablespoon instant coffee and 1 teaspoon ground cinnamon to sweetened condensed milk. Proceed as above.

Butterscotch Fudge: Omit chocolate chips and vanilla. In heavy saucepan, melt 2 (12-ounce) packages butterscotch flavored chips with sweetened condensed milk. Remove from heat; stir in 2 tablespoons white vinegar, ⅛ teaspoon salt, ½ teaspoon maple flavoring and 1 cup chopped nuts. Proceed as above.

CREAMY WHITE FUDGE

Makes about 2¼ pounds

1½ pounds white confectioners' coating*
1 (14-ounce) can Eagle® Brand Sweetened Condensed Milk (NOT evaporated milk)
⅛ teaspoon salt
¾ to 1 cup chopped nuts
1½ teaspoons vanilla extract

In heavy saucepan, over low heat, melt coating with sweetened condensed milk and salt. Remove from heat; stir in nuts and vanilla. Spread evenly into wax paper-lined 8- or 9-inch square pan. Chill 2 hours or until firm. Turn fudge onto cutting board; peel off paper and cut into squares. Store tightly covered at room temperature.

MICROWAVE: In 2-quart glass measure, combine coating, sweetened condensed milk and salt. Microwave on full power (high) 3 to 5 minutes or until coating melts, stirring after 3 minutes. Stir in vanilla and nuts. Proceed as above.

Praline Fudge: Omit vanilla. Add 1 teaspoon maple flavoring and 1 cup chopped pecans. Proceed as above.

Confetti Fudge: Omit nuts. Add 1 cup chopped mixed candied fruit. Proceed as above.

Rum Raisin Fudge: Omit vanilla. Add 1½ teaspoons white vinegar, 1 teaspoon rum flavoring and ¾ cup raisins. Proceed as above.

Cherry Fudge: Omit nuts. Add 1 cup chopped candied cherries.

*White confectioners' coating can be purchased in candy specialty stores.

To make Strawberry Bon Bons, form mixture into strawberry shapes; coat with gelatin.

Use pastry bag with open star tip to pipe green frosting onto strawberries to form stems.

FRUIT BON BONS

Makes about 5 dozen

1 (14-ounce) can Eagle® Brand Sweetened Condensed Milk (NOT evaporated milk)
2 (7-ounce) packages flaked coconut (5⅓ cups)
1 (6-ounce) package fruit flavor gelatin, any flavor
1 cup ground blanched almonds
1 teaspoon almond extract
Food coloring, optional

In large mixing bowl, combine sweetened condensed milk, coconut, ⅓ cup gelatin, almonds, extract and enough food coloring to tint mixture desired shade. Chill 1 hour or until firm enough to handle. Using about ½ tablespoon mixture for each, shape into 1-inch balls. Sprinkle remaining gelatin onto wax paper; roll each ball in gelatin to coat. Place on wax paper-lined baking sheets; chill. Store covered at room temperature or in refrigerator.

Strawberry Bon Bons: Using strawberry flavor gelatin, prepare bon bon mixture as above. Form into strawberry shapes. In small bowl, combine 2¼ cups sifted confectioners' sugar, 3 tablespoons whipping cream and few drops green food coloring. Using pastry bag with open star tip, pipe small amount on top each strawberry.

LAYERED MINT CHOCOLATE CANDY

Makes about 1¾ pounds

1 (12-ounce) package semi-sweet chocolate chips
1 (14-ounce) can Eagle® Brand Sweetened Condensed Milk (NOT evaporated milk)
2 teaspoons vanilla extract
6 ounces white confectioners' coating*
1 tablespoon peppermint extract
Few drops green or red food coloring, optional

In heavy saucepan, over low heat, melt chips with 1 cup sweetened condensed milk. Stir in vanilla. Spread half the mixture into wax paper-lined 8- or 9-inch square pan; chill 10 minutes or until firm. Hold remaining chocolate mixture at room temperature. In heavy saucepan, over low heat, melt coating with remaining sweetened condensed milk. Stir in peppermint extract and food coloring if desired. Spread on chilled chocolate layer; chill 10 minutes longer or until firm. Spread reserved chocolate mixture on mint layer. Chill 2 hours or until firm. Turn onto cutting board; peel off paper and cut into squares. Store loosely covered at room temperature.

*White confectioners' coating can be purchased in candy specialty stores.

MILK CHOCOLATE BOURBON BALLS

Makes about 5½ dozen

1 (12-ounce) package vanilla
    wafer cookies, finely crushed
    (about 3 cups crumbs)
5 tablespoons bourbon or brandy
1 (11½-ounce) package milk
    chocolate chips
1 (14-ounce) can Eagle® Brand
    Sweetened Condensed Milk
    (NOT evaporated milk)
Finely chopped nuts

In medium mixing bowl, combine crumbs and bourbon. In heavy saucepan, over low heat, melt chips. Remove from heat; add sweetened condensed milk. Gradually add crumb mixture; mix well. Let stand at room temperature 30 minutes or chill. Shape into 1-inch balls; roll in nuts. Store tightly covered.

Tip: Flavor of these candies improves after 24 hours. They can be made ahead and stored in freezer.

BUCKEYES

Makes about 7 dozen

2 (3-ounce) packages cream
    cheese, softened
1 (14-ounce) can Eagle® Brand
    Sweetened Condensed Milk
    (NOT evaporated milk)
2 (12-ounce) packages peanut
    butter flavored chips
1 cup finely chopped peanuts
1 (6-ounce) package semi-sweet
    chocolate chips
1 square (1 ounce) paraffin wax
    or 2 tablespoons shortening

In large mixer bowl, beat cheese until fluffy. Gradually beat in sweetened condensed milk until smooth. In heavy saucepan, over low heat, melt peanut butter chips; stir into cheese mixture. Add nuts. Chill 2 to 3 hours; shape into 1-inch balls. In small heavy saucepan, over low heat, melt chocolate chips with paraffin. With wooden pick, dip each peanut ball into chocolate mixture, not coating completely. Place on wax paper-lined baking sheets until firm. Store covered at room temperature or in refrigerator.

COCONUT RUM BALLS

Makes about 8 dozen

1 (12-ounce) package vanilla
    wafer cookies, finely crushed
    (about 3 cups crumbs)
1 (3½-ounce) can flaked coconut
    (1⅓ cups)
1 cup finely chopped nuts
1 (14-ounce) can Eagle® Brand
    Sweetened Condensed Milk
    (NOT evaporated milk)
¼ cup rum
    Additional flaked coconut or
    confectioners' sugar

In large mixing bowl, combine crumbs, coconut and nuts. Add sweetened condensed milk and rum; mix well. Chill 4 hours. Shape into 1-inch balls. Roll in coconut. Store tightly covered in refrigerator.

Tip: Flavor of these candies improves after 24 hours. They can be made ahead and stored in refrigerator for several weeks.

CHOCOLATE PECAN CRITTERS

Makes about 5 dozen

1 (11½-ounce) package milk
    chocolate chips
1 (6-ounce) package semi-sweet
    chocolate chips
¼ cup margarine or butter
1 (14-ounce) can Eagle® Brand
    Sweetened Condensed Milk
    (NOT evaporated milk)
⅛ teaspoon salt
2 cups coarsely chopped pecans
2 teaspoons vanilla extract
    Pecan halves

In heavy saucepan, over medium heat, melt chips and margarine with sweetened condensed milk and salt. Remove from heat; stir in nuts and vanilla. Drop by teaspoonfuls onto wax paper-lined baking sheets. Top with pecan halves. Chill. Store tightly covered.

MICROWAVE: In 2-quart glass measure, microwave chips, margarine, sweetened condensed milk and salt on full power (high) 3 minutes. Stir after 1½ minutes. Stir to melt chips; stir in remaining ingredients. Proceed as above.

PEANUT BUTTER LOGS

Makes two 12-inch logs

**1 (12-ounce) package peanut
  butter flavored chips**
**1 (14-ounce) can Eagle® Brand
  Sweetened Condensed Milk
  (NOT evaporated milk)**
**1 cup Campfire® Miniature
  Marshmallows**
1 cup chopped peanuts

In heavy saucepan, over low heat, melt
chips with sweetened condensed milk.
Add marshmallows; stir until melted.
Remove from heat; cool 20 minutes.
Divide in half; place each portion on a
20-inch piece of wax paper. Shape
each into 12-inch log. Roll in nuts. Wrap
tightly; chill 2 hours or until firm.
Remove paper; cut into ¼-inch slices.

MICROWAVE: In 2-quart glass measure,
microwave chips, sweetened condensed milk and marshmallows on full
power (high) 4 minutes or until melted,
stirring after 2 minutes. Let stand at
room temperature 1 hour.

Peanut Butter Fudge: Stir peanuts into
mixture. Spread into wax paper-lined 8-
or 9-inch square pan. Chill 2 hours or
until firm. Turn fudge onto cutting board;
peel off paper and cut into squares.

GOLDEN SNACKING GRANOLA

Makes about 2½ quarts

2 cups oats
**1½ cups slivered almonds or
  coarsely chopped walnuts**
**1 (3½-ounce) can flaked coconut
  (1⅓ cups)**
½ cup sunflower meats
½ cup wheat germ
2 tablespoons sesame seeds
1 teaspoon ground cinnamon
1 teaspoon salt
**1 (14-ounce) can Eagle® Brand
  Sweetened Condensed Milk
  (NOT evaporated milk)**
¼ cup vegetable oil
1 cup banana chips, optional
1 cup raisins

Preheat oven to 300°. In large mixing
bowl, combine all ingredients except
banana chips and raisins; mix well.
Spread evenly in aluminum foil-lined
15x10-inch jellyroll pan or baking
sheet. Bake 55 to 60 minutes, stirring
every 15 minutes. Remove from oven;
stir in banana chips and raisins. Cool
thoroughly. Store tightly covered at
room temperature.

Golden Snacking Granola

GINGER ORANGE NUT BALLS

Makes about 8 dozen

1 (16-ounce) package ginger
   snap cookies, finely crushed
   (about 4 cups crumbs)
1 (14-ounce) can Eagle® Brand
   Sweetened Condensed Milk
   (NOT evaporated milk)
1 (3½-ounce) can flaked coconut
   (1⅓ cups)
1 cup finely chopped nuts
1 cup raisins
⅓ cup orange juice
1 tablespoon grated orange rind
   Additional flaked coconut and
   grated orange rind

In large mixing bowl, combine all
ingredients except additional coconut
and rind. Chill at least 1 hour. Shape
into 1-inch balls. Roll in additional
coconut mixed with rind. Store tightly
covered in refrigerator.

Tip: Flavor of these candies improves
after 24 hours. They can be made
ahead and stored in refrigerator for
several weeks.

EASY PEANUT BUTTER CHOCOLATE FUDGE

Makes about 2 pounds

1 (12-ounce) package peanut
   butter flavored chips
¼ cup margarine or butter
1 (14-ounce) can Eagle® Brand
   Sweetened Condensed Milk
   (NOT evaporated milk)
½ cup chopped peanuts, optional
1 (6-ounce) package semi-sweet
   chocolate chips

In heavy saucepan, melt peanut butter
chips and 2 *tablespoons* margarine with
1 *cup* sweetened condensed milk.
Remove from heat; stir in nuts. Spread
into wax paper-lined 8-inch square pan.
In small heavy saucepan, melt chocolate chips and remaining 2 *tablespoons*
margarine with remaining sweetened
condensed milk. Spread chocolate
mixture on top of peanut butter mixture.
Chill 2 hours or until firm. Turn fudge
onto cutting board; peel off paper and
cut into squares. Store loosely covered
at room temperature.

CHOCOLATE FRUIT BALLS

Makes about 10 dozen

2½ cups vanilla wafer crumbs
    (about 65 wafers)
1 (14-ounce) can Eagle® Brand
    Sweetened Condensed Milk
    (NOT evaporated milk)
1 (8-ounce) package chopped
    dates
1 cup finely chopped nuts
½ cup chopped candied cherries
2 tablespoons unsweetened
    cocoa
    Confectioners' sugar or
    unsweetened cocoa
    Additional candied cherries,
    optional

In large mixing bowl, combine all
ingredients except confectioners'
sugar and additional cherries; mix well.
Chill 1 hour. Shape into 1-inch balls.
Roll in confectioners' sugar. Store
tightly covered in refrigerator. Garnish
with additional candied cherries if
desired.

Tip: Flavor of these candies improves
after 24 hours. They can be made
ahead and stored in refrigerator for
several weeks.

SCOTCHY TURTLES

Makes about 5 dozen

1 (6-ounce) package butter-
    scotch flavored chips
1 (14-ounce) can Eagle® Brand
    Sweetened Condensed Milk
    (NOT evaporated milk)
2 teaspoons white vinegar
4 cups pecan halves (¾ pound)
1 (11½-ounce) package milk
    chocolate chips
1 teaspoon vanilla extract

In heavy saucepan, over low heat, melt
butterscotch chips with ⅓ cup sweetened condensed milk. Remove from
heat; stir in vinegar. Drop by half
teaspoonfuls onto wax paper-lined
baking sheets. Arrange 3 pecans on
each butterscotch drop. In large heavy
saucepan, over low heat, melt milk
chocolate chips with remaining sweetened condensed milk and vanilla.
Remove from heat; hold chocolate
mixture over hot water. Drop chocolate
by heaping teaspoonfuls over pecan
clusters. Chill 2 hours or until firm.
Store loosely covered.

MICROWAVE: In 1-quart glass measure,
combine butterscotch chips and ⅓ cup
sweetened condensed milk. Microwave
on full power (high) 1½ minutes. Stir to
melt chips. Add vinegar. Proceed as
above. In 1-quart glass measure,
combine milk chocolate chips with
remaining sweetened condensed milk.
Microwave on full power (high) 2
minutes. Stir to melt chips. Add vanilla.
Proceed as above.

CHOCOLATE TRUFFLES

Makes about 6 dozen

3 (6-ounce) packages semi-sweet chocolate chips
1 (14-ounce) can Eagle® Brand Sweetened Condensed Milk (NOT evaporated milk)
1 tablespoon vanilla extract
Finely chopped nuts, flaked coconut, chocolate sprinkles, colored sprinkles, unsweetened cocoa *or* colored sugar

In heavy saucepan, over low heat, melt chips with sweetened condensed milk. Remove from heat; stir in vanilla. Chill 2 hours or until firm. Shape into 1-inch balls; roll in any of the above coatings. Chill 1 hour or until firm. Store covered at room temperature.

MICROWAVE: In 1-quart glass measure, combine chips and sweetened condensed milk. Microwave on full power (high) 3 minutes, stirring after 1½ minutes. Stir until smooth. Proceed as above.

Amaretto: Omit vanilla. Add 3 tablespoons amaretto or other almond-flavored liqueur and ½ teaspoon almond extract. Roll in finely chopped toasted almonds.

Orange: Omit vanilla. Add 3 tablespoons orange-flavored liqueur. Roll in finely chopped toasted almonds mixed with finely grated orange rind.

Rum: Omit vanilla. Add ¼ cup dark rum. Roll in flaked coconut.

Bourbon: Omit vanilla. Add 3 tablespoons bourbon. Roll in finely chopped toasted nuts.

CHOCOLATE CHERRY LOGS ▶

Makes two 12-inch logs

3 (6-ounce) packages semi-
    sweet chocolate chips
1 (14-ounce) can Eagle® Brand
    Sweetened Condensed Milk
    (NOT evaporated milk)
1 (6-ounce) container candied
    cherries, chopped (about
    1 cup)
1 teaspoon almond extract
1½ cups slivered almonds, toasted
    and chopped

In heavy saucepan, over low heat, melt
chips with sweetened condensed milk.
Remove from heat. Stir in cherries and
extract. Chill 30 minutes. Divide in half;
place each portion on a 20-inch piece
of wax paper. Shape each into 12-inch
log. Roll in nuts. Wrap tightly; chill
2 hours or until firm. Remove paper; cut
into ¼-inch slices to serve. Store
covered in refrigerator.

MICROWAVE: In 2-quart glass measure,
combine chips and sweetened condensed milk. Microwave on full power
(high) 3 minutes, stirring after 1½
minutes. Stir in cherries and extract.
Chill 1 hour. Proceed as above.

TOASTED VIENNA CHUNKS

Makes about 5 dozen

½ loaf Vienna or French bread,
    cut into 1-inch cubes
1 (14-ounce) can Eagle® Brand
    Sweetened Condensed Milk
    (NOT evaporated milk)
1 (7-ounce) package flaked
    coconut (2⅔ cups)

Preheat oven to 350°. Dip bread into
sweetened condensed milk; allow to
drain briefly. Roll in coconut. Place on
aluminum foil-lined and greased baking
sheets; bake 8 minutes or until coconut
is toasted. *Immediately* remove from
baking sheets. Store loosely covered at
room temperature.

Tip: For a campfire treat, toast chunks
over open fire.

ROCKY ROAD CANDY

Makes about 3½ dozen

1 (12-ounce) package semi-
    sweet chocolate chips
2 tablespoons margarine or
    butter
1 (14-ounce) can Eagle® Brand
    Sweetened Condensed Milk
    (NOT evaporated milk)
2 cups dry roasted peanuts
1 (10½-ounce) package Camp-
    fire® Miniature Marshmallows

In heavy saucepan, over low heat, melt
chips and margarine with sweetened
condensed milk; remove from heat. In
large mixing bowl, combine nuts and
marshmallows; stir in chocolate mixture.
Spread in wax paper-lined 13x9-inch
pan. Chill 2 hours or until firm. Remove
from pan; peel off wax paper and cut
into squares. Store loosely covered at
room temperature.

MICROWAVE: In 1-quart glass measure,
combine chips, margarine and sweetened condensed milk. Microwave on
full power (high) 3 minutes, stirring
after 1½ minutes. Stir to melt chips. Let
stand 5 minutes. Proceed as above.

CARAMEL PEANUT BALLS

Makes about 4½ dozen

3 cups *finely* chopped dry
    roasted peanuts
1 (14-ounce) can Eagle® Brand
    Sweetened Condensed Milk
    (NOT evaporated milk)
1 teaspoon vanilla extract
1 (6-ounce) package semi-sweet
    chocolate chips
1 square (1 ounce) paraffin wax
    or 2 tablespoons shortening

In heavy saucepan, combine nuts,
sweetened condensed milk and vanilla.
Over medium heat, cook and stir 8 to
10 minutes or until mixture forms ball
around spoon and pulls away from side
of pan. Cool 10 minutes. Chill if desired.
Shape into 1-inch balls. In small heavy
saucepan, over low heat, melt chips
with paraffin. With wooden pick, dip
each ball into chocolate mixture, coating
half of ball. Place on wax paper-lined
baking sheets until firm. Store covered
at room temperature or in refrigerator.

CHIPPER PEANUT CANDY

Makes about 2 pounds

1 (14-ounce) can Eagle® Brand
    Sweetened Condensed Milk
    (NOT evaporated milk)
1 (6-ounce) package butter-
    scotch flavored chips
1 cup peanut butter
2 cups crushed potato chips
1 cup coarsely chopped peanuts

In heavy saucepan, melt butterscotch
chips with sweetened condensed milk
and peanut butter. Over medium heat,
cook and stir until well blended.
Remove from heat. Add potato chips
and nuts; mix well. Press into aluminum
foil-lined 8- or 9-inch square pan. Chill.
Turn candy onto cutting board; peel off
foil and cut into squares. Store loosely
covered at room temperature.

MICROWAVE: In 2-quart glass measure,
combine sweetened condensed milk,
butterscotch chips and peanut butter.
Microwave on full power (high) 4
minutes, stirring after 2 minutes.
Proceed as above.

CRUNCHY CLUSTERS

Makes about 3 dozen

1 (12-ounce) package semi-
    sweet chocolate chips *or*
    3 (6-ounce) packages
    butterscotch flavored chips
1 (14-ounce) can Eagle® Brand
    Sweetened Condensed Milk
    (NOT evaporated milk)
1 (3-ounce) can chow mein
    noodles *or* 2 cups pretzel
    sticks, broken into ½-inch
    pieces
1 cup dry roasted peanuts *or*
    whole roasted almonds

In heavy saucepan, over low heat, melt
chips with sweetened condensed milk.
Remove from heat. In large mixing
bowl, combine noodles and nuts; stir in
chocolate mixture. Drop by tablespoon-
fuls onto wax paper-lined baking
sheets; chill 2 hours or until firm. Store
loosely covered in cool dry place.

MICROWAVE: In 2-quart glass measure,
combine chips and sweetened condensed milk. Microwave on full power
(high) 3 minutes, stirring after 1½
minutes. Stir until smooth. Proceed as
above.

APRICOT ALMOND CHEWIES

Makes about 6½ dozen

4 cups finely chopped dried
    apricots (about 1 pound)
4 cups flaked coconut or coconut
    macaroon crumbs (about 21
    macaroons)
2 cups slivered almonds, toasted
    and finely chopped
1 (14-ounce) can Eagle® Brand
    Sweetened Condensed Milk
    (NOT evaporated milk)
    Whole almonds, optional

In large mixing bowl, combine all
ingredients except whole almonds.
Chill 2 hours. Shape into 1-inch balls.
Top each with whole almond if desired.
Store tightly covered in refrigerator.

Pictured Top to Bottom: Apricot Almond
Chewies, Chipper Peanut Candy, Caramel
Peanut Balls, Crunchy Clusters—Butterscotch
and Chocolate, Chipper Peanut Candy.

Pictured: Orange Pineapple Punch (recipe page 114).

BEVERAGES

FROM THE DESSERT MAKER

ORANGE PINEAPPLE PUNCH

Makes about 4 quarts

1 (46-ounce) can pineapple
  juice, chilled
1½ cups light rum, optional
1 (14-ounce) can Eagle® Brand
  Sweetened Condensed Milk
  (NOT evaporated milk)
1 (6-ounce) can frozen orange
  juice concentrate, thawed
2 (32-ounce) bottles ginger ale,
  chilled
  **Orange sherbet, orange slices
  and mint leaves**

In large punch bowl, combine all
ingredients except ginger ale and
sherbet. Just before serving, gradually
add ginger ale; stir. Top with scoops of
sherbet, orange slices and mint.

CREAMY PINK PUNCH

Makes about 3½ quarts

2 (14-ounce) cans Eagle® Brand
  Sweetened Condensed Milk
  (NOT evaporated milk)
1 to 1½ cups kirsch or other
  cherry-flavored liqueur
¼ cup grenadine syrup
2 (32-ounce) bottles club soda,
  chilled
  Cherry vanilla ice cream

In large punch bowl, combine sweetened condensed milk, kirsch and
grenadine. Just before serving,
gradually add club soda; stir. Top
with scoops of ice cream.

CREAMY HOT CHOCOLATE

Makes about 2 quarts

1 (14-ounce) can Eagle® Brand
  Sweetened Condensed Milk
  (NOT evaporated milk)
½ cup unsweetened cocoa
1½ teaspoons vanilla extract
⅛ teaspoon salt
6½ cups hot water
  Marshmallows, optional

In large saucepan, combine sweetened
condensed milk, cocoa, vanilla and salt;
mix well. Over medium heat, slowly stir
in water; heat through, stirring
occasionally. DO NOT BOIL. Top with
marshmallows if desired.

MICROWAVE: In 2-quart glass measure,
combine all ingredients except marshmallows. Microwave on full power
(high) 8 to 10 minutes, stirring every
3 minutes. Top with marshmallows if
desired.

Tip: Chocolate can be stored in
refrigerator up to 5 days. Mix well and
reheat before serving.

Creamy Hot Chocolate

BANANA SHAKE

Makes about 5 cups

2 ripe bananas, cut up (about 2 cups)
1 (14-ounce) can Eagle® Brand Sweetened Condensed Milk (NOT evaporated milk)
1 cup cold water
⅓ cup ReaLemon® Lemon Juice from Concentrate
2 cups ice cubes

In blender container, combine all ingredients except ice; blend well. Gradually add ice, blending until smooth. Garnish as desired. Refrigerate leftovers. (Mixture stays thick and creamy in refrigerator.)

Strawberry: Omit bananas. Add 1 pint fresh strawberries, cleaned and hulled *or* 2 cups frozen unsweetened strawberries, partially thawed and few drops red food coloring if desired. Proceed as above.

Orange-Banana: Omit 1 banana and reduce ReaLemon to ¼ cup. Add 1 (6-ounce) can frozen orange juice concentrate, thawed. Proceed as above.

Pineapple: Omit bananas. Add 1 (8-ounce) can crushed juice-packed pineapple. Proceed as above.

MIXER METHOD: Omit ice cubes. In large mixer bowl, mash fruit; gradually beat in ReaLemon, sweetened condensed milk and 2½ cups cold water. Chill before serving.

Pictured: Strawberry Shake, Banana Shake.

GRASSHOPPER PUNCH

Makes about 2½ quarts

**1 (14-ounce) can Eagle® Brand
Sweetened Condensed Milk
(NOT evaporated milk)
½ cup green creme de menthe
½ cup white creme de cacao
2 (32-ounce) bottles club soda,
chilled
Mint chocolate chip ice cream**

In punch bowl, combine sweetened
condensed milk, creme de menthe and
creme de cacao; mix well. Slowly pour
in club soda. Top with scoops of ice
cream.

COFFEE EGG NOG PUNCH

Makes about 1½ quarts

**3 cups cold milk
1 (14-ounce) can Eagle® Brand
Sweetened Condensed Milk
(NOT evaporated milk)
4 eggs*
3 to 4 teaspoons instant coffee
⅓ cup bourbon
⅓ cup coffee-flavored liqueur
1 cup (½ pint) whipping cream,
whipped
Dash ground cinnamon
Dash ground nutmeg**

In large mixer bowl, combine milk,
sweetened condensed milk, eggs and
coffee; beat on low speed until coffee
dissolves. Stir in bourbon and liqueur;
chill. Before serving, top with whipped
cream, cinnamon and nutmeg.
Refrigerate leftovers.

Holiday Egg Nog: Omit instant coffee
and coffee-flavored liqueur. Increase
bourbon to ½ cup; add 1 teaspoon
vanilla extract. Proceed as above.

*Use only Grade A clean, uncracked
eggs.

BRANDY MILK PUNCH

Makes about 3 quarts

**5 cups cold milk
2 (14-ounce) cans Eagle® Brand
Sweetened Condensed Milk
(NOT evaporated milk)
1 to 1½ cups brandy
1 cup light rum
3 egg whites*
Nutmeg**

In large punch bowl, combine milk and
sweetened condensd milk; add brandy
and rum. In small bowl, beat egg whites
to soft peaks. Stir into milk mixture.
Chill. Garnish with nutmeg. Refrigerate
leftovers.

*Use only Grade A clean, uncracked
eggs.

HOMEMADE CREAM LIQUEUR

Makes about 1 quart

1 (14-ounce) can Eagle® Brand Sweetened Condensed Milk (NOT evaporated milk)
1¼ cups flavored liqueur (almond, coffee, orange *or* mint)
1 cup (½ pint) whipping or coffee cream
4 eggs*

In blender container, combine all ingredients; blend until smooth. Serve over ice and garnish if desired. Store tightly covered in refrigerator up to 1 month. Stir before serving.

MIXER METHOD: In large mixer bowl, beat eggs; beat in remaining ingredients until smooth and well blended. Proceed as above.

*Use only Grade A clean, uncracked eggs.

HOMEMADE IRISH CREAM LIQUEUR

Makes about 5 cups

1¾ cups liquor (Irish whiskey, brandy, rum, bourbon, scotch *or* rye whiskey)
1 (14-ounce) can Eagle® Brand Sweetened Condensed Milk (NOT evaporated milk)
1 cup (½ pint) whipping or coffee cream
4 eggs*
2 tablespoons chocolate flavored syrup
2 teaspoons instant coffee
1 teaspoon vanilla extract
½ teaspoon almond extract

In blender container, combine all ingredients; blend until smooth. Serve over ice if desired. Store tightly covered in refrigerator up to 1 month. Stir before serving.

MIXER METHOD: In large mixer bowl, beat eggs; beat in remaining ingredients until smooth and well blended. Proceed as above.

Dessert Making Hints

INTRODUCTION

Eagle Brand is an all-natural concentrated blend of whole milk and cane sugar condensed by a special vacuum cooking process. It is entirely different from evaporated milk. Eagle Brand may become thicker and more caramel-colored as its age or storage temperature increases. The performance of the product is not affected by these natural changes. The grocer's shelf life indicated on the can is 15 months. However, the unopened product is safe and wholesome indefinitely as long as the can seal is intact. If the sweetened condensed milk becomes unusually thick, stir briskly before using. If the product has become very carmelized, use in recipes where the caramel flavor is compatible with other ingredients. The best storage for sweetened condensed milk is a cool, dry place.

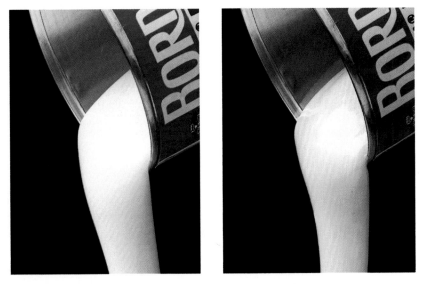

Because it is a natural product, Eagle Brand may vary in color and consistency from can to can. These two photos illustrate the normal differences which may occur in Eagle Brand over time.

HINTS FOR USING EAGLE BRAND

- Remove entire end of can with can opener; then use rubber scraper to remove all of the sweetened condensed milk from the can.
- To avoid lumps in a cream cheese base recipe, gradually beat sweetened condensed milk into beaten cream cheese.
- Always heat sweetened condensed milk and chocolate over low or medium heat, stirring constantly.
- To avoid lumpy gelatine mixtures, sprinkle unflavored gelatine over cold water; let stand 1 minute. Cook and stir over *low* heat until dissolved.
- Always store any unused sweetened condensed milk in refrigerator in covered container. Use within a week.

EAGLE BRAND IS PRESWEETENED

Because Eagle Brand contains sugar which has already been thoroughly dissolved in the manufacturing process, most Eagle Brand recipes require no additional sugar.

EAGLE BRAND & CHOCOLATE

When heated with chocolate, Eagle Brand quickly thickens to a velvety smooth consistency for candies and sauces that are never grainy or long-cooking. There's no need for constant stirring or a candy thermometer.

MAGIC THICKENING

Because it is a precooked blend of milk and sugar, Eagle Brand thickens almost magically with the addition of acidic fruit juices—to form delicious pie fillings, puddings and desserts *without cooking.* Lemon juice or orange juice concentrate works best.

ICE CREAM MAKING

The thick creamy consistency of Eagle Brand helps to minimize the formation of large ice crystals in ice creams and frozen desserts.

A NOTE ABOUT EGGS

Some recipes in this book specify, "Use only Grade A clean, uncracked eggs." This is a precaution given when un-cooked eggs are called for—egg nog, meringues, pie fillings, etc.

HOW TO CARAMELIZE EAGLE BRAND

Oven Method: Preheat oven to 425°. Pour 1 (14-ounce) can Eagle® Brand Sweetened Condensed Milk into 8- or 9-inch pie plate. Cover with aluminum foil; place in shallow pan. Fill pan with hot water. Bake 1 to 1½ hours or until thick and light caramel-colored. Remove foil; cool. Chill thoroughly. Refrigerate leftovers.

Stovetop Method: Pour 1 (14-ounce) can Eagle® Brand Sweetened Condensed Milk into top of double boiler; cover. Place over boiling water. Simmer 1 to 1½ hours or until thick and light caramel-colored. Beat until smooth. Cool. Chill thoroughly. Refrigerate leftovers.

Serve caramelized sweetened condensed milk with fruit, chopped nuts, whipped cream or shaved chocolate.

*CAUTION: NEVER HEAT UNOPENED CAN.

CRUMB CRUST

Makes one 8- or 9-inch crust

**1½ cups graham cracker or
    chocolate wafer crumbs
¼ cup sugar
6 tablespoons margarine or
    butter, melted**

Combine ingredients; mix well. Press firmly on bottom and up side to rim of 8- or 9-inch pie plate. Chill thoroughly or bake in preheated 375° oven 6 to 8 minutes or until edges are brown. Cool before filling.

PASTRY CRUST

Makes one 8- or 9-inch crust

**1 cup unsifted flour
½ teaspoon salt
⅓ cup shortening
3 to 4 tablespoons cold water**

In medium mixing bowl, combine flour and salt; cut in shortening until mixture resembles coarse corn meal.Sprinkle with water, 1 tablespoon at a time, mixing until dough is just moist enough to hold together. Form dough into ball. Place on well-floured surface. Press down into a flat circle with smooth edges. Roll dough to a circle ⅛-inch thick and about 1½ inches larger than inverted pie plate. Ease dough into pie plate. Trim ½ inch beyond pie plate edge. Fold under; flute edge as desired.

TO BAKE WITHOUT FILLING ▶

Preheat oven to 450°. Prick bottom and side of pastry shell with fork. Line pastry with aluminum foil; fill with dry beans. Bake 5 minutes; remove beans and foil. Bake 5 to 7 minutes longer or until golden.

TO BAKE WITH FILLING

Preheat oven as directed in recipe. Do not prick pastry shell. Fill and bake as directed.

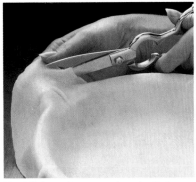

Use kitchen shears or sharp knife to trim dough ½ inch beyond pie plate edge. Fold under extra dough to form rim.

Flute edge as desired.

To keep an unfilled pastry crust from puffing or shrinking during baking, line with aluminum foil and fill with dry beans.

FOR SUCCESSFUL MERINGUE

- Weather affects meringues. When the humidity is high, the sugar in the meringue absorbs moisture from the air, making the meringue gooey and limp. Meringues should be made on sunny, dry days.
- Carefully separate egg whites from the yolks (they separate best when cold).
- Mixing bowls and beaters should be completely grease-free.
- Egg whites should come to room temperature before beating. This increases the volume.
- Sugar should be added *gradually*. Continue beating until sugar is completely dissolved.

Continued next column

For Successful Meringue

- Cool meringue slowly, away from drafts to prevent shrinking and weeping.

MERINGUE

For 8- or 9-inch pie

3 egg whites
¼ teaspoon cream of tartar
6 tablespoons sugar

Preheat oven to 350°. In small mixer bowl, beat egg whites with cream of tartar until soft peaks form; gradually add sugar, beating until stiff but not dry. Spread meringue on top of pie, sealing carefully to edge of pastry shell. Bake 12 to 15 minutes or until golden brown. Cool. Chill thoroughly.

1. Beat egg whites and cream of tartar to *soft peaks* before adding sugar.

2. *Gradually* add sugar, beating until *stiff* but not dry. Mixture should be glossy.

3. Spread meringue, sealing carefully to edge of pastry shell.

4. Brown meringue as directed. Cool *slowly.*

121

TINTING COCONUT

Dilute few drops food coloring with
½ teaspoon water or milk. Add coconut;
toss with fork until evenly tinted.

TOASTING COCONUT AND NUTS

Spread coconut or nuts evenly in
shallow pan. Toast in preheated 350°
oven 7 to 15 minutes or until golden,
stirring frequently.

FROSTING GRAPES

Dip small clusters of grapes into slightly
beaten egg white; sprinkle with granulated sugar. Dry on wire racks.

CHOCOLATE LEAVES

Coat undersides of real leaves lightly
with vegetable oil. Melt semi-sweet
chocolate and coat undersides of
leaves thickly with chocolate using
small spoon. Chill or freeze until firm,
then peel away leaf.

CHOCOLATE CURLS

With a vegetable parer or thin, sharp
knife, slice across block of sweet milk
chocolate or large-size milk chocolate
candy bar with long, thin strokes.
Chocolate should be at room
temperature.

PASTRY EGG WASH

For a more golden crust on a 2-crust
pie, beat 1 egg yolk with 2 tablespoons
water; brush evenly over pastry before
baking.

To split cake layer, measure halfway up
side; mark with toothpicks. Using long
piece of thread, rest on picks. Cross
thread and pull through to split layers.

For level layers, use a long thin serrated
knife to slice off rounded or uneven top
of cake.

MAKE-AHEAD WHIPPED CREAM

Freeze dollops of whipped cream on wax paper-lined baking sheets. When frozen, store in tightly closed plastic bags for use on desserts or Irish coffee.

FOR BAKED ALASKAS

Ice cream must be very firm before it is covered with meringue and baked. Dessert can be frozen several days before serving.

UNMOLDING FROZEN DESSERTS

For easy unmolding of ice cream desserts, line container with aluminum foil, extending foil beyond rim of container. When frozen, lift dessert from pan with foil.

To marble, gently swirl a narrow spatula through the light and dark mixtures.

SLICING HINTS

- Use a wet knife for cutting desserts with meringue. Wipe off knife after each cut.
- Use a damp knife with a thin blade for slicing cake rolls.
- Use a damp knife with a firm blade for cutting fudge or candy.
- Use a serrated knife for slicing angel food cakes.

WHIPPING CREAM ▶

- Chill beaters and bowl thoroughly.
- Beat chilled whipping cream on high speed (overbeating or beating on low speed can cause cream to separate into fat and liquid).
- Beat only until stiff. Whipping cream doubles in volume.
- To sweeten whipped cream, gradually beat in 1 to 2 tablespoons granulated or confectioners' sugar and $1/2$ to 1 teaspoon vanilla extract for each cup unwhipped whipping cream.

Beat whipping cream only until *stiff* peaks form.

INDEX

G

E

H

I

F

PUDDINGS

Q

R

S

SAUCES/TOPPINGS

T

V

Y

CLASSIC DESSERTS RECIPE BOOK

Here's how to get your copy—an $8.95 retail value!
☐ Send $3.95 plus 2 proofs of purchase   OR
☐ Send $5.95 with no proofs of purchase

Check appropriate box and mail your
check or money order with your name,
address, city, state and zip to:

"CLASSIC DESSERTS"
P.O. Box 7073
Clinton, Iowa 52736

NAME_____

ADDRESS_____

CITY_____

STATE_____ ZIP_____

Allow 6 weeks for delivery. Offer good only in U.S.A. Void where restricted.

‒ ‒ ‒ ‒ ‒ ‒ ‒ ‒ ‒ ‒ ‒ ‒ ‒ ‒ ‒ ‒ ‒ ‒ ‒ ‒

CLASSIC DESSERTS RECIPE BOOK

Here's how to get your copy—an $8.95 retail value!
☐ Send $3.95 plus 2 proofs of purchase   OR
☐ Send $5.95 with no proofs of purchase

Check appropriate box and mail your
check or money order with your name,
address, city, state and zip to:

"CLASSIC DESSERTS"
P.O. Box 7073
Clinton, Iowa 52736

NAME_____

ADDRESS_____

CITY_____

STATE_____ ZIP_____

Allow 6 weeks for delivery. Offer good only in U.S.A. Void where restricted.

‒ ‒ ‒ ‒ ‒ ‒ ‒ ‒ ‒ ‒ ‒ ‒ ‒ ‒ ‒ ‒ ‒ ‒ ‒ ‒

CLASSIC DESSERTS RECIPE BOOK

Here's how to get your copy—an $8.95 retail value!
☐ Send $3.95 plus 2 proofs of purchase   OR
☐ Send $5.95 with no proofs of purchase

Check appropriate box and mail your
check or money order with your name,
address, city, state and zip to:

"CLASSIC DESSERTS"
P.O. Box 7073
Clinton, Iowa 52736

NAME_____

ADDRESS_____

CITY_____

STATE_____ ZIP_____

Allow 6 weeks for delivery. Offer good only in U.S.A. Void where restricted.

‒ ‒ ‒ ‒ ‒ ‒ ‒ ‒ ‒ ‒ ‒ ‒ ‒ ‒ ‒ ‒ ‒ ‒ ‒ ‒

CLASSIC DESSERTS RECIPE BOOK

Here's how to get your copy—an $8.95 retail value!
☐ Send $3.95 plus 2 proofs of purchase   OR
☐ Send $5.95 with no proofs of purchase

Check appropriate box and mail your
check or money order with your name,
address, city, state and zip to:

"CLASSIC DESSERTS"
P.O. Box 7073
Clinton, Iowa 52736

NAME_____

ADDRESS_____

CITY_____

STATE_____ ZIP_____

Allow 6 weeks for delivery. Offer good only in U.S.A. Void where restricted.